# HOW TO GET OVER A BREAKUP AND MOVE ON

*Heal Your Heart, Rebuild Your Confidence, and Create a Life You Love After a Relationship Ends*

*By Sophie Hartman*

Published by Edenroot Press
**edenrootpress.com**

EDENROOT
PRESS

# Contents

# ♥ About Sophie Hartman

**Sophie Hartman** is an internationally recognised relationship coach, bestselling author, and emotional wellness expert whose mission is to help people create healthier, more connected, and deeply fulfilling relationships.

With over 15 years of experience guiding individuals and couples around the world, Sophie blends practical strategies with deep emotional insight to help her readers and clients overcome dating struggles, heal emotional wounds, improve communication, and rediscover intimacy that lasts.

Her work is grounded in the belief that **everyone deserves to feel loved, heard, and emotionally safe, starting with themselves.** Whether you're navigating heartbreak, struggling with trust, or simply want to connect more deeply with the people around you, Sophie's gentle, evidence-backed approach offers guidance that's both healing and empowering.

Through her growing collection of bestselling books and digital resources, Sophie has reached tens of thousands of readers with one core message:

💬 *You don't have to settle for painful relationships. You can build better ones, and it starts with you.* every woman who's ever questioned her worth because of love

# Acknowledgements

Writing this book was an act of healing, not just for you, the reader, but also for me.

Because the truth is, I don't write these words from some untouched mountaintop of perfect love or unshakable confidence. I write them from lived experience. From the messy, tender middle. From the heartbreaks that taught me who I really am. And from the quiet, powerful decision to grow instead of shut down.

To the brave souls who shared their stories with me, clients, friends, readers, and strangers, you are the heartbeat of this book. Thank you for trusting me with your truth, your pain, your questions, and your hope. You reminded me that healing is universal, but also beautifully personal.

To my readers, whether this is your first book of mine or your sixth, I'm deeply honoured to walk beside you. Thank you for letting my words into the intimate corners of your life. You are the reason I keep writing.

To the friends and chosen family who showed up for me during my own heartbreaks, with tea, texts, hugs, and zero judgment, thank you. Your presence helped me rediscover my own light, one day at a time.

To the loves I've lost: thank you. Not because it didn't hurt, it did. But because every ending shaped me. Every goodbye returned me to myself. Every lesson helped me write this book, not from theory, but from truth.

And finally, to *you*, reading this right now:

Thank you for showing up for your healing. For choosing to keep your heart open, even after it broke. For doing the deep, tender, brave work of letting go and moving forward.

Your courage is nothing short of sacred.

With endless gratitude,
**Sophie Hartman**

# Chapter 1: The Shock of Letting Go

There's a moment after a breakup, sometimes it hits you the same day, other times it sneaks in days or weeks later, when the truth finally sinks in.

It's over.

You stare at your phone, fingers hovering over their contact, still half-expecting a message. You roll over in bed and instinctively reach out for someone who's not there. You walk down the street and for a second forget, then remember, and the remembering knocks the wind out of you all over again.

The silence can be deafening. The world feels blurry. You're still breathing, still standing, but everything feels different.

That's the shock of letting go.

And it's not just in your head. It's in your body, your nervous system, your heart. Breakups hit like emotional earthquakes, leaving cracks you never expected, shaking foundations you thought were solid. Even when the relationship wasn't perfect. Even when *you were the one who ended it*. Even when you *knew* deep down it needed to end.

Because losing someone you loved, or once imagined a future with, hurts, no matter the circumstances.

Let's talk about why.

---

## The Emotional Chaos After a Breakup

In the days or weeks after a breakup, most people feel like they're riding an emotional rollercoaster they never bought a ticket for. One minute you're crying into your cereal, the next you're fine, until something triggers you again, and suddenly you're back in the pit of despair. You might feel:

- Disoriented, like nothing makes sense

- Numb, as if your emotions have turned off completely

- Panicked, desperate to "fix it" or get them back

- Angry, at them, at yourself, at everything

- Or completely stuck, unable to move forward or backward

It can feel like you're falling apart. But here's what I want you to know: **this chaos is normal**.

You're not going crazy. You're grieving.

---

## The Psychology of Heartbreak

Let's talk science for a second. Love, especially romantic attachment, activates some of the same brain systems as addiction. When you're in a close relationship, your brain releases a powerful cocktail of bonding hormones like oxytocin, dopamine, and serotonin. You grow accustomed to this emotional feedback loop of connection, safety, and validation.

So when the relationship ends? Your brain doesn't just switch off those patterns. It *panics*. It goes into withdrawal.

That's why you might find yourself obsessively checking their social media, replaying conversations, or fantasising about reconciliation. Your nervous system is literally looking for its next "hit" of comfort, even if the relationship was painful or unfulfilling.

Add to that the sense of lost identity (Who am I without this person?), the collapse of future plans (We were supposed to travel this fall…), and the natural human resistance to change, and you've got a full-blown emotional storm.

You are grieving a loss. Just because the person is still alive doesn't mean it's not a death of sorts.

## The Grief Cycle of Love Lost

Many people don't realise that breakups often follow the same emotional arc as bereavement. Elisabeth Kübler-Ross's five stages of grief, denial, anger, bargaining, depression, acceptance, apply here, too. Not in a neat, linear order, but in messy waves.

Let's break that down:

- **Denial**: *"This can't really be over. They'll text. We'll work it out."*

- **Anger**: *"How could they do this? Why didn't they fight for us?"*

- **Bargaining**: *"If I change, maybe they'll come back. Maybe I was the problem."*

- **Depression**: *"I can't believe it's really over. I feel empty."*

- **Acceptance**: *"It hurts, but I know this is the right path forward."*

You may cycle through these more than once. You may get stuck in one for weeks, then leap forward unexpectedly. That's okay. There is no right way to grieve the end of a relationship.

But there is something profoundly healing in understanding *that you are grieving*. This isn't just emotional weakness. It's a deeply human process.

---

## You're Not Broken , You're Human

When you're in the depths of heartbreak, it's easy to judge yourself. "I should be stronger." "I should be over this by now." "Why do I care so much?"

Pause. Breathe. Let's rewrite that narrative.

You're not weak for feeling this way. You're not broken. You're not overreacting. You're not pathetic.

**You're processing a loss.**

Of love. Of comfort. Of familiarity. Of hopes and dreams. Maybe even of the version of yourself that existed in that relationship.

And all of that deserves tenderness.

There is no expiration date on pain. There is no shame in grief. The only thing to do is walk through it, slowly, compassionately, and with support.

## Story: When It Feels Like You'll Never Get Over It

Let me introduce you to *Rachel*. Not her real name, but her very real story.

Rachel had been with her partner for almost five years. They'd met in college, built a life together, talked about marriage, even adopted a dog. When the relationship started to unravel, Rachel was in denial. She kept trying to fix it, to shrink herself, to hold it all together.

But eventually, he left.

Rachel was devastated. She cried every day for months. She couldn't eat. Couldn't sleep. Her friends stopped knowing what to say. She thought, "What if this is it? What if I never feel okay again?"

But slowly, with time, therapy, journaling, and self-compassion, Rachel began to rebuild.

She discovered painting. She started hiking again. She made new friends. She travelled solo to a place she'd always wanted to visit. One day, almost without realising it, she went a full day without thinking about him. And then a week.

Now, years later, she says something powerful: "That breakup felt like the end of my world. But it turned out to be the beginning of finding myself."

You don't need to believe this today. But I want you to know, Rachel's story is not rare. Most people think they won't survive a breakup until they do.

And not only survive, but *grow*.

---

## What You're Feeling Is Temporary

Right now, you may feel like you're drowning in emotions. But emotions are like waves, they rise, they peak, and eventually, they recede.

This pain will not last forever.

Let me repeat that: **This pain will not last forever**.

You will breathe easier again. You will laugh without it catching in your throat. You will walk into places without scanning the crowd for them. You will fall asleep without replaying every word they said. You will stop needing closure from them, because you'll find it within yourself.

It doesn't mean you won't carry the memory. It doesn't mean you'll forget what you shared. But the sting will soften. The intensity will fade. And one day, this chapter will simply be part of your story, not the whole book.

## Gentle Reminders and Takeaways

Let's ground this chapter with a few truths to hold close:

- **Breakups trigger a real grieving process.** You are not "too sensitive", you are experiencing loss.

- **It's normal to feel disoriented, desperate, or numb.** You're not failing at healing. This is part of it.

- **What you're feeling is human, and temporary.** This moment is not your forever.

So if your heart feels heavy right now, if your mind keeps spinning with what-ifs, if your body aches with the absence of someone who used to feel like home, I see you.

You are not alone.

And this? This is just the beginning of your healing.

## A Note Before We Go On...

You don't need to rush through this chapter or "solve" your pain before you move forward in the book. Let each page meet you where you are. If today you're just trying to make it to bedtime without texting them, *that counts*. If you're staring at this chapter with tears in your eyes, wondering if you'll ever feel like *you* again, *you will*.

Give yourself permission to grieve.

You're letting go of more than a person. You're letting go of a version of life you thought would be yours. And that's a sacred process.

But trust me: what's coming will not just fill the empty space, they'll build something new, something more aligned with who you're becoming.

You are healing.

Even now.

Even here.

# Chapter 2: Was It Really That Perfect?

Heartbreak has a funny way of polishing the past. Like an old photo softened by time, our memories of the relationship can start to blur, edges smoothed, colours brightened, flaws quietly erased.

You find yourself remembering how they laughed at your jokes. How they held you when you were falling apart. The late-night talks. The morning coffee routine. That one weekend when everything felt easy and perfect.

And suddenly, you're spiralling: *Why did we break up? Was it really that bad? Did I make a mistake? What if I just focused on the negatives and now I've thrown away something rare?*

If this sounds familiar, take a breath. What you're experiencing is normal. And it has a name.

---

## When the Brain Tells Half the Story

After a breakup, your brain starts looking for comfort. And comfort often comes in the form of *nostalgia*, a sweet, warm lens that makes everything in the past seem shinier than it was.

But nostalgia is *selective memory*.

When we're hurting, we tend to focus on the good times because they provide relief. The brain often edits out the hard parts. It's a psychological phenomenon known as **cognitive dissonance**, your mind struggling to reconcile the pain of now with the imagined perfection of then.

Here's how it plays out:

- You remember the cuddles, not the cold silences

- The holidays together, not the emotional distance

- The fun inside jokes, not the deep incompatibilities

- The physical connection, not the constant miscommunication

Your brain wants to protect you from pain. But sometimes, it does so by distorting the truth.

And that can keep you stuck.

## You Can Miss Them *And* Know They Weren't Right for You

Let's break a myth: *Missing someone doesn't mean they were meant for you.*

You can miss someone and still recognise that the relationship wasn't healthy. You can love aspects of who they were and still acknowledge that your needs weren't being met. You can feel sad, lonely, and regretful, and still be making the right decision by letting go.

Love is not always enough. And longing is not the same as compatibility.

Sometimes we hold on to the idea of a person, not the person themselves. We fall in love with potential. With what it *could have been*. With the early days, the promises, the occasional moments of connection that made us *hope* things could get better.

But hope, when clung to at the expense of reality, becomes a trap.

---

## Rewriting the Story With Honesty

Let me ask you a few questions, and I want you to answer them with radical honesty:

- Were you consistently emotionally safe in this relationship?

- Could you fully express your needs without fear or shutdown?

- Did you feel deeply seen, respected, and prioritised?

- Were issues truly resolved, or just swept under the rug repeatedly?

- Did you have to betray parts of yourself to keep the peace?

If your gut clenches reading those, that's not a failure. That's *information*.

So often, we replay highlight reels in our mind while ignoring the full movie. But healing requires truth. And truth requires looking at the whole picture, not just the pretty parts.

---

## Story: The Perfect Illusion

Let me tell you about *David*. After his girlfriend broke up with him, David was convinced he'd lost the love of his life. He called her his soulmate. He replayed every good memory they shared, her laugh, their road trips, the way she used to surprise him with handwritten notes.

But in therapy, something unexpected happened. As he started unpacking the relationship, other memories surfaced. The times she dismissed his anxiety. The way she flirted with others in front of him and then gaslighted him for being "too sensitive." The constant cycle of apology and blame.

Eventually, David realised he hadn't been in love with who she was, he'd been in love with who he *wanted* her to be. And the loss he felt wasn't just about her, it was about letting go of the fantasy.

That insight was painful. But it was also the turning point.

David's healing began the day he started telling himself the *whole* story.

---

## The Relationship Reality Check

Let's make this tangible. Below is an exercise you can try right now or return to later when you feel ready. This is your **Relationship Reality Check**.

### Step 1: The Highlight Reel
Write down 5 of your favourite memories from the relationship. Let yourself feel the warmth. Acknowledge

the joy. Honour what was good, this is not about erasing the positives.

### Step 2: The Full Picture
Now write down 5 memories or patterns that caused pain, discomfort, or left you feeling unseen or small. Be honest. These don't have to be big explosive fights, sometimes the most damaging parts are the subtle ones that chipped away at your self-worth over time.

### Step 3: Contrast & Truth
Read both lists. Sit with the contrast. Then answer:

- Which list reflects the day-to-day experience more accurately?

- Did the good times outweigh the hard times, or were they just louder?

- What did you *have* in this relationship, and what was consistently *missing*?

This is not about punishing yourself or your ex. It's about clarity.

Because clarity gives you power.

---

# Pain Can Distort Perception

When we're heartbroken, we don't always want truth, we want comfort. And sometimes, the comfort comes from romanticising the person who hurt us. But here's the gentle truth:

- They may have loved you, but still not treated you well.

- You may have loved them, but still not felt loved in return.

- There may have been beautiful moments, but not a healthy foundation.

We're complex. Relationships are complex. And holding both the good and the bad at once is what maturity looks like.

But if you keep only replaying the good, you risk walking backwards, toward someone who may no longer align with the person you're becoming.

---

## Let's Be Clear...

This isn't about demonising your ex or rewriting the story to say everything was awful. Most relationships aren't all bad or all good, they live in the grey.

This is about balance.

Truth is the foundation of healing. When you can look at the relationship with both eyes open, with compassion and clarity, you take back your power. You see the *real* story, not the one edited by grief or loneliness.

And from that place, you get to write a new story. For you.

---

## Takeaways to Hold Onto

Here's what I want you to remember today:

- **You can miss someone and still know they weren't right for you.**

- **Pain distorts perception, truth restores clarity.**

- **Healing begins when we stop telling ourselves half the story.**

You don't have to rush. This process will take time, and you'll probably find yourself slipping back into rose-tinted memories now and then. That's okay. When it happens, gently remind yourself: *I'm remembering part of the story, not the whole one.*

And when you're ready, choose truth. Every time you do, you heal a little more.

## Coming Up Next...

In the next chapter, we'll explore a tough question: *Why did it end, even if you didn't want it to?* We'll move beyond obsessing over closure and focus on honest understanding, so you can stop spinning in circles and start moving forward.

You're doing brave, hard, beautiful work. Keep going. I'm right here with you.

# Chapter 3: Why It Ended (Even If You Didn't Want It To)

One of the most painful realities of heartbreak is this: **sometimes, you didn't want the ending.**

You weren't ready. You weren't the one who called it off. You were still fighting. Still believing. Still holding on to the thread of hope that maybe, just maybe, things could work out.

But it ended anyway.

And now, you're left with a thousand questions and almost no satisfying answers.

Your mind spins: *What did I miss? Could I have done something differently? Was it me? Was it them? Did I expect too much? Was I not enough? Was it just bad timing? Could this still be fixed?*

The ache of not understanding *why* something ended can sometimes hurt more than the ending itself. And so, you search. You analyse. You replay every conversation, every argument, every sign.

This is what we do when we crave closure.

But let's talk about a hard truth: **some breakups don't come with a clean explanation.**

And yet, that doesn't mean you can't find peace.

---

## Not All Endings Come With Closure

We're wired for meaning. The human brain *needs* to make sense of things, especially emotionally painful things. A breakup without clarity can feel like an open wound that won't heal. That's why we chase closure, we think if we just *understand*, we can finally let go.

But here's the twist: **chasing closure from someone else rarely brings the relief we hope for.** Because what we're often asking for isn't just truth, it's comfort. We want the other person to make our pain make sense. To explain it in a way that soothes our heart.

And when that doesn't happen, or when their answer still doesn't feel like *enough*, we start obsessing.

We over-analyse. We turn ourselves into detectives of our own heartbreak. We look for patterns, read old texts, ask friends to dissect every detail. But that kind of analysis often just deepens the pain.

Understanding *why* something ended is important, but *only* when it's done with compassion, not self-blame. With curiosity, not desperation.

So let's take a breath, and approach this with honesty and kindness.

# Why Do Relationships End? (Even When There's Love)

Let's demystify the breakup question. Most relationships don't end for just *one* reason. They unravel over time, in small ways, in quiet cracks, in slow drifting. And often, both people play a part.

Here are some of the most common reasons relationships end, even when love is present:

## 1. Incompatibility

You can care deeply about someone and still not be a good long-term fit. Values clash. Communication styles don't align. One of you wants kids, the other doesn't. You love differently. You fight in ways that hurt instead of heal. These things matter more than we often admit.

## 2. Unmet Needs

Maybe your emotional needs were dismissed. Maybe theirs were. Maybe you needed more affection, more reassurance, more stability, and it never came. Maybe you silenced your needs to keep the peace, but resentment grew. Needs that go unmet don't just disappear. They become wounds.

## 3. Betrayal

This could be infidelity. It could be broken promises, lies, or emotional abandonment. Betrayal can fracture trust so deeply that the relationship can't recover, even if both people want to try.

## 4. Drift

This is the slow, painful ending. No blow-up. No betrayal. Just the realisation that you've become strangers to each other. That you've grown in different directions. That the connection that once felt electric now feels... absent.

And then sometimes, it just *stops working*. There's no explosion, just exhaustion.

---

## A Loving Inventory (Without Blame)

Here's what I want you to understand: **every relationship is co-created.** It's not all your fault. It's not all theirs, either. You both brought your history, your wounds, your fears, your patterns. You both tried in the ways you knew how. And maybe that still wasn't enough.

But that doesn't mean *you* weren't enough.

Let's ask some gentle questions. Not to over-analyse, but to *understand*:

- Did I feel emotionally safe in this relationship?

- Did I feel heard and valued when I expressed a need?

- Did we repair conflict well, or did issues stay unresolved?

- Were we both invested equally in growth?

- Did I shrink parts of myself to stay?

These aren't questions to judge yourself. They're questions to help you see clearly. Because **clarity gives peace, not punishment.**

---

## Story: When It Doesn't Make Sense, Yet

Let's talk about *Alyssa*. She was in a three-year relationship that ended suddenly. One day they were planning a trip together, the next, he said he "wasn't happy anymore" and left.

Alyssa was blindsided. For months she spiralled, replaying every conversation. She stalked his social media. She even considered texting his sister to try to "understand" what happened.

But the truth? He never gave a clear reason. And no answer she invented ever truly helped.

In therapy, Alyssa started shifting her questions.

Instead of *"Why did he leave?"*, she began asking, *"What did I feel in this relationship that I ignored?"*

She remembered how often she felt lonely, even when he was next to her. How she was always trying to "earn" his affection. How she stayed silent about her needs out of fear he'd pull away.

That shift, from obsessing over *his* motives to understanding *her* truth, was the turning point.

Alyssa didn't get external closure. She gave it to herself.

---

## Stop Looking for One Big "Why"

Here's something I see all the time: people searching for *one* reason the breakup happened. The one moment it fell apart. The one thing they did wrong. The one red flag they missed.

But relationships aren't that tidy.

They're complex, messy, layered. They end for many reasons, and sometimes, there's no clean narrative.

And here's the real truth: **closure doesn't come from the perfect answer. It comes from self-trust.**

When you learn to trust that you can survive the not-knowing… when you stop needing *them* to explain your pain in order for you to heal… that's when you reclaim your power.

---

## Let Go of the Labels

One of the ways we try to make sense of breakups is by labelling them.

- *"It was a toxic relationship."*

- *"They were a narcissist."*

- *"I was codependent."*

- *"They were emotionally unavailable."*

Sometimes those labels are helpful. They give us language. They validate our pain.

But be careful, because labels can also become cages. They can keep you locked in the story, analysing it instead of *releasing* it. They can fuel resentment, or worse, self-blame disguised as insight.

You don't need to name every psychological dynamic to know this:

**It wasn't working. And you deserve more.**

Let that be enough for now.

---

## Takeaways to Ground You

If this chapter stirred things up, here are a few truths to hold on to:

- **Closure comes from understanding, not obsessing.** Stop chasing a neat ending and start exploring what *you* need to heal.

- **Not all breakups come with satisfying answers.** And that's okay. You can still move forward without one.

- **Focus on lessons, not labels.** What did you learn? What will you choose differently next time?

And most of all, remember this:

You are not defined by the ending of this relationship. You are defined by how you *rise* from it.

## Looking Ahead…

In the next chapter, we're going to talk about something difficult but essential: the emotional addiction that often follows a breakup. Why missing someone feels like withdrawal. Why "just one text" can set you back weeks. And how to break the cycle, so you can start healing clearly and cleanly.

This is not the end of your story.

It's the moment you start writing the next chapter, one where *you* are at the centre.

You're doing beautifully. Keep going.

# Chapter 4: Breaking the Emotional Addiction

You know that moment. The one where you swear you're doing better, stronger, clearer, and then suddenly, you're reaching for your phone. Just to check their Instagram. Just to scroll through old photos. Just to see if they maybe, possibly, miraculously texted you.

And when they haven't? You feel it, the ache. The longing. The familiar panic.

And when they *have*? You feel... hope. Confusion. A flicker of excitement... followed quickly by emotional whiplash.

This, my love, is the emotional addiction of a breakup. And it's *real*.

---

## Love and Attachment as Neurological Bonds

Let's get one thing straight: the bond you had with your ex wasn't just emotional, it was *neurological*.

When we fall in love, attach deeply, or feel emotionally bonded to someone, our brain releases powerful chemicals, oxytocin (bonding), dopamine (pleasure/reward), serotonin (stability), and more. These create a biochemical connection, especially when there's regular affection, routine, intimacy, and shared vulnerability.

Over time, your nervous system starts to associate that person with safety, comfort, relief, and reward. They become your emotional *home base.*

So what happens when that home is suddenly gone?

You go into *withdrawal,* just like with any other addictive pattern.

---

## Withdrawal Isn't Just Psychological, It's Physical

Missing them can feel like a real, physical ache. You might experience:

- Racing thoughts

- Irritability or anxiety

- Restlessness

- A tight chest or upset stomach

- A desperate urge to reach out

- Deep emotional lows followed by high moments of hope

This isn't weakness. This is *neurology*. Your brain is screaming, *"Where is my fix? Where is my reward? Where is my comfort?"*

It's no different than trying to quit caffeine, nicotine, or sugar, except now the craving is tied to someone who knows exactly how to light up your brain's pleasure centres.

The truth? **You're not weak, you're detoxing.**

---

## Missing Them Doesn't Mean You Should Go Back

Let's pause here and say something clearly:

**Missing someone does not mean they were right for you.**

It does not mean the relationship was healthy.

It does not mean you should reconnect.

All it means is that your system is adjusting to an absence. The same way your body misses sugar when you give it up, even though you know it wasn't serving you.

The danger comes when we mistake withdrawal for a sign that we "shouldn't have ended it" or "still love them deeply." When in truth, **what you're feeling is the bond loosening, and your brain resisting that loss**.

But loosening is exactly what needs to happen.

---

## The False Hope Loop

If you're caught in the on-again, off-again cycle with your ex, this is important. That loop of break up → reconnect → heartbreak again → repeat? That's textbook addiction behaviour.

You keep returning because:

- There's a hit of emotional reward (dopamine) when they reach out

- Your brain confuses familiarity with safety

- You hope "maybe this time will be different"

- You fear the discomfort of total loss

But each reconnection just reinforces the neurological bond, and resets the withdrawal clock. That's why "just one message" can feel like you've been emotionally reset by weeks or months.

To truly heal, you need to **break the loop**.

And that begins with something most people resist, but is absolutely essential.

---

## The Power of No Contact

I know. It sounds harsh. It sounds cold. It sounds extreme.

But hear me out.

**No contact is not about punishment. It's about protection.**

It's not a game. It's not about proving anything to them. It's about giving *yourself* the space, time, and emotional silence you need to detach fully, neurologically, emotionally, physically.

Because as long as they have access to you, your thoughts, your heart, your inbox, your healing will be delayed.

Imagine trying to quit sugar while still licking lollipops. That's what "staying in touch" feels like to your nervous system.

So what does *no contact* really mean?

---

## Tool Tip: The No Contact Roadmap

Here's a simple guide to support your emotional detox.

### 🔒 Step 1: Define Your Boundaries

- **No texting, calling, or DMing** them (even for closure, even for "just checking in")

- **Mute or block** them on social media (you don't need constant emotional exposure)

- **Remove their number** or at least rename it to something like "Do Not Contact"

- **Delete old conversations**, or at minimum, archive them

- If you share logistics (e.g., kids, pets), limit contact strictly to that topic and use neutral language

### ☐ Step 2: Manage the Cravings

When the urge hits:

- **Set a timer**: Wait 20 minutes before doing anything. Let the wave pass.

- **Do a nervous system reset**: Try deep breathing, movement, or cold water.

- **Reach out to someone safe**: A friend who reminds you why you left.

- **Journal the craving**: "Right now I want to text them because…"

- **Remind yourself**: "This is withdrawal. This will pass."

### 🦷 Step 3: Replace the Fix

Detachment isn't just about stopping the old, it's about *replacing* it.

- Create *new routines* (coffee shop you've never been to, different route to work)

- Invest in *connection with others* (even when you don't feel like it)

- Channel your energy into healing habits: movement, therapy, creativity, learning

- Say yes to *yourself* more often, rest, boundaries, self-kindness

---

## You Need Time and Space to Heal Clearly

If you've ever tried to see your reflection in muddy water, you know what it's like to try to heal while staying emotionally entangled with someone who hurt you.

You can't heal clearly when they're still in your head, your feed, or your inbox.

Clarity requires stillness.

It requires enough emotional distance to remember who *you* are outside of them.

It requires detox.

And yes, it's hard at first. You'll feel raw. You'll feel restless. You'll second-guess yourself.

But if you stay the course, if you commit to space, you will *feel the fog start to lift*.

And that's when the real healing begins.

---

## Story: From Looping to Liberation

Let me introduce you to *Kevin*. He broke up with his ex after years of emotional push-pull. Every time he left, she would reel him back in with messages like, *"I miss you"* or *"Can we talk?"* And every time, Kevin returned, hopeful, vulnerable… and soon, heartbroken again.

Eventually, he decided to try 30 days of no contact. It was brutal. He checked his phone constantly. He cried in the car. He journaled obsessively. But he *stuck with it*.

By week three, something shifted. He started sleeping better. He started feeling anger, not just pain. He began remembering the moments he'd ignored or excused. And for the first time, he saw the full truth of the relationship, not the fantasy.

That 30 days turned into 60. Then 90. And by then, Kevin didn't *want* to go back. He didn't need her to explain anything. He had found his peace.

No contact didn't erase the love. But it gave him something more valuable: **freedom**.

---

## Takeaways to Ground You

Let's wrap this chapter with the truths you need to carry with you:

- **Missing them doesn't mean you should go back.** It means your nervous system is adjusting.

- **Emotional detox is real, and necessary.** The pain of withdrawal is temporary.

- **You need time and space to heal clearly.** Boundaries aren't cruelty. They're clarity.

You don't have to do this perfectly. You just have to *choose yourself*, one quiet, strong moment at a time.

---

## Looking Ahead...

In the next chapter, we're going to soften. You'll learn how to actually *feel* your feelings without drowning in them. Why grief needs expression, not suppression, and how to create space for your pain to move through you, rather than stay stuck inside.

You are doing brave, honest work right now. Keep showing up. You're getting stronger with every page.

# Chapter 5: Making Space for Your Emotions

There's a moment in every healing journey where the numbness wears off… and the pain sets in.

You're going about your day, maybe folding laundry, driving home, or trying to make small talk at work, and suddenly, it hits. The lump in your throat. The sting in your eyes. The tightness in your chest.

Sometimes it's grief. Sometimes it's rage. Sometimes it's that heavy fog of sadness that just won't lift.

And your first instinct? Shut it down.

*"Don't cry here." "Just keep busy." "You should be over this by now." "Stop being dramatic."*

We've been taught to fear our emotions, especially the messy, inconvenient ones. But here's the truth most people never tell you:

**You can't heal what you won't feel.**

If you want to move forward, you have to stop stuffing the pain into a corner. You have to make space for it, so it can finally move through you.

---

## Why Suppressing Pain Backfires

Suppressing emotions might work in the short term. You get through your workday. You smile in front of your kids. You make it through dinner without crying.

But feelings don't disappear just because you ignore them. They go underground. And there, they build pressure, showing up as anxiety, irritability, insomnia, emotional numbness, or even physical pain.

Your body keeps the score. Your nervous system remembers what you suppress.

And sooner or later, those buried emotions find a way to surface. Sometimes in the quiet of night. Sometimes in explosive reactions to small things. Sometimes in complete emotional burnout.

**Pain that is buried alive doesn't die, it festers.**

---

## Feeling Fully Without Drowning

Let's be clear: making space for your emotions doesn't mean you have to cry all day or sit in sadness for hours.

It means allowing the emotion to exist.

Letting it rise.

Acknowledging it without shame.

And then giving it a place to go.

Think of emotions like waves. They rise, they crest, and they fall. But if you panic and fight the wave, you drown. If you let yourself ride it, stay present, breathe through it, it eventually carries you back to shore.

Here's what feeling fully might look like:

- Taking five minutes in your car to let yourself sob

- Writing a letter to your ex you'll never send

- Screaming into a pillow when the anger is unbearable

- Saying out loud, *"I miss them, and this hurts so much"*

- Sitting quietly and letting a single tear fall

These are not signs of weakness. These are *acts of emotional courage.*

---

## The Difference Between Processing and Wallowing

Some people avoid their emotions because they're afraid of getting *stuck* in them. They confuse *processing* with *wallowing*.

Let's make the distinction:

- **Processing** is conscious. You're allowing emotions to rise so you can understand them, release them, and move forward.

- **Wallowing** is passive. You're replaying the pain without intention, using it to punish yourself or feed hopelessness.

The key difference? **Intention.**

Processing sounds like:
*"I'm feeling intense grief today, so I'm going to journal, cry, and be gentle with myself."*

Wallowing sounds like:
*"I'll never get over this. I was stupid to think I could be happy. I deserve this pain."*

One leads to healing. The other deepens suffering.

And if you ever find yourself wallowing? Don't shame yourself. Just notice it. Name it. And gently ask, *"What do I actually need right now?"*

## Emotions Heal When They're Felt

You don't have to analyse every feeling. You don't have to understand *why* you're sad before you allow yourself to be sad.

Your job isn't to fix your feelings, it's to *feel* them.

When you cry, you're not falling apart. You're *releasing*.

When you feel anger, you're not broken. You're *validating* that something mattered.

When you miss them, it doesn't mean you want them back. It means you're *human*.

And emotions, like all natural processes, are *meant to move*. But they need your permission to do so.

Give your grief a safe container. A journal. A walk. A voice note to yourself. A playlist that understands your heart.

Make space, and you'll be amazed at how your emotions begin to soften.

---

## Story: The Closet Cry That Changed Everything

Let me tell you about *Brittany*. After her fiancé broke off their engagement, Brittany tried to stay strong. She went to work, stayed social, posted positive quotes on Instagram.

But behind closed doors, she was exhausted. Numb. Unwell. Every time she felt the tears coming, she'd distract herself with something, Netflix, cleaning, scrolling.

Until one afternoon, she walked into her bedroom, closed the closet door, and sank to the floor.

And she let it out.

All of it. The sobbing. The shaking. The "why me?" questions. The ugly, messy, raw heartbreak.

And afterward?

She felt *relief*. Not fixed. Not happy. But lighter. Clearer. *Real.*

She told me later, "I think I started healing the moment I let myself fall apart."

---

## Emotional Healing Is Not Linear

Some days you'll feel okay. Others you won't. Sometimes you'll cry less, then randomly spiral. You might think you're past it, only to hear *your song* in a store and end up back in tears.

This is not failure. This is grief.

You are *not* going backwards.

You are *not* broken.

You are *processing*.

Healing doesn't happen in perfect little steps. It loops. It stumbles. It rests. It rises.

Your only job is to keep showing up for yourself in it.

To stay gentle. To stay honest. To stay willing to feel what you feel.

Because every time you do, you loosen pain's grip just a little more.

---

## Takeaways to Hold Close

Let's anchor this chapter with a few loving truths:

- **Emotions heal when they're felt, not avoided.**

- **Crying is not weakness, it's release.**

- **Emotional healing is not linear.** It's messy, non-linear, and entirely human.

So today, if you feel like crying, cry.

If you feel like screaming, scream.

If you feel nothing, honour that, too.

Whatever comes up, meet it with compassion. You're not too emotional. You're not too much. You're not failing.

You are feeling. And that is healing.

---

## Looking Ahead...

In the next chapter, we'll talk about *guilt* and the heavy weight of the "what ifs." We'll unpack why regret shows up after a breakup, how to release self-blame, and why perfectionism has no place in love.

Keep breathing. Keep trusting. You're walking through the hardest parts right now, and your future self is already so proud of you.

# Chapter 6: The Guilt and the 'What Ifs'

*What if I had just been more patient?*
*What if I didn't say that one thing?*
*What if I had fought harder... or walked away sooner...*
*or loved them better?*
*What if I ruined the best thing I ever had?*

If you've asked yourself any version of those questions lately, you're not alone.

One of the heaviest emotions we carry after a breakup isn't sadness or anger, it's **guilt**.

Not just for what happened, but for what we think we *should have done differently*.

We rewind the tape, looking for the pivotal moment we "messed it up." We pick ourselves apart, our choices, our words, our patterns, and try to find the version of ourselves that would've made the relationship work.

But guilt doesn't always tell the truth.

And when left unchecked, it can keep us locked in shame... instead of healing with compassion.

---

## Why Guilt Shows Up

Guilt is a complex emotion. Sometimes, it's healthy. It tells us when we've crossed a boundary, hurt someone we care about, or acted out of alignment with our values. In those cases, guilt is a guide, it helps us grow.

But after a breakup, guilt often shows up *not because you've done something wrong*, but because:

- You lost something you valued

- You feel powerless and want to make sense of it

- You're trying to regain a sense of control

- You've Internalised messages that love is your responsibility to "get right"

And so the mind creates a fantasy: *If I had just done X, this wouldn't have happened.*

It's a soothing lie.

Because if it was *your fault*, then maybe you can *fix it*. Maybe you can go back in time, rewrite the script, get a different ending.

But that story doesn't bring peace. It brings self-punishment.

---

## Letting Go of Perfectionism in Love

Here's the truth no one tells you: **even the best, kindest, most self-aware version of you could not have saved a relationship that wasn't meant to last.**

Love isn't a performance. And relationships aren't exams you can ace with enough preparation and effort.

Perfectionism in love sounds like:

- *"If I had communicated better, we wouldn't have fought."*

- *"If I were less emotional, they'd still be here."*

- *"I should have been more understanding, more secure, more… everything."*

But love doesn't work like that. You can't contort yourself into someone worthy of being chosen. You can't control another person's ability to show up, stay, or meet you halfway.

You're not a robot. You're a human being in a relationship with *another* human being. Which means…

**You're not responsible for doing it perfectly.**

You're responsible for *being real*, for growing, for showing up honestly, and yes, sometimes imperfectly.

And that's enough.

---

## Relationships Are Co-Created

Let's be clear: **you didn't break this relationship all by yourself.** You didn't make it hard all by yourself. And you couldn't have saved it all by yourself either.

All relationships are co-created. That means the good moments? Shared. The breakdowns? Shared. The outcome? Shared.

Even if your partner never admitted fault.

Even if you were the one who always tried to repair.

Even if they blamed you entirely.

This isn't about absolving yourself of responsibility. It's about remembering that **your responsibility ends where theirs begins**.

Your ex had choices. They had agency. They had patterns and flaws and limits too.

You are not the sole architect of this ending.

---

## Story: The Weight She Didn't Deserve

Let me tell you about *Maria*. She came to me after ending a two-year relationship where she always felt "not enough." Her partner constantly told her she was too emotional, too needy, too sensitive.

After the breakup, Maria spiralled into guilt. She told me, "If I had just stayed calm. If I had just not been so reactive. Maybe he wouldn't have left."

But as we worked together, we began looking deeper.

Maria had been consistently dismissed. Her needs were invalidated. She'd walk on eggshells just to avoid his cold silence. The more she tried to "fix herself," the more emotionally abandoned she became.

Eventually, she realised: she wasn't the problem. She was the one *trying*. She just didn't have a partner who was willing, or able, to meet her halfway.

Maria's guilt began to soften. And in its place? Came grief. Then self-forgiveness. Then power.

She had done her best with what she knew. And now? She was ready to do better, *for herself.*

---

## Releasing the Fantasy of Control

One of the hidden roots of guilt is the fantasy that we could've controlled the outcome.

We imagine ourselves saying the "right thing," staying calmer, being more accommodating… and magically, the relationship survives.

This fantasy isn't just comforting, it's seductive. Because if *we* were the problem, then *we* can be the solution.

But real life doesn't work that way.

People leave for their own reasons. Relationships end for reasons that go beyond words, beyond logic, beyond control.

Sometimes you outgrow each other.
 Sometimes your trauma responses clashed.
 Sometimes one or both of you just didn't have the tools to do better.

That's not failure.

That's life.

---

## You Did the Best You Could With What You Knew

Let this land in your heart:

**You did the best you could with the awareness, tools, and self-worth you had at the time.**

Could you do it differently now? Maybe. But you didn't *have* the clarity then that you do now. And *that* matters.

Growth means looking back and saying, *"I understand why I did what I did. And I'm choosing to learn from it, not shame myself for it."*

This is how we honour our past *and* evolve.

This is how we heal.

---

## Takeaways to Ground You

Let's hold onto these truths:

- **You did the best you could with what you knew.** That's enough.

- **Relationships are co-created, not single-handedly saved.** It wasn't just on you.

- **Growth comes from compassion, not criticism.** You don't need to punish yourself to become better.

Your job now is to release the guilt, stop rewriting the past, and come home to self-forgiveness.

Because blame won't heal you. But love, starting with love for yourself, can.

---

## Looking Ahead...

In the next chapter, we'll explore what it means to heal from *betrayal*, whether that's infidelity, dishonesty, or emotional abandonment. We'll talk about how to rebuild trust in *yourself* again, and how to let go without needing apology or revenge.

You are not broken.

You are becoming wiser, braver, and more grounded with every truth you face.

And that is something to be proud of.

# Chapter 7: Healing from Betrayal or Loss of Trust

There are breakups… and then there are **breaks in trust**.

The kind that leave you questioning not just the relationship, but *everything*.

*Was any of it real?*
*How could they do this?*
*Did I not matter?*
*Why didn't I see it coming?*
*How will I ever trust again?*

Whether it was **infidelity**, **chronic dishonesty**, **emotional abandonment**, or another betrayal of your safety , this kind of pain cuts deeper. It's not just the loss of a person. It's the shattering of something sacred: *trust*.

And when trust breaks, it doesn't just hurt. It disorients.

You don't just lose them, you start to lose pieces of *yourself*. Your confidence. Your clarity. Your sense of what's true.

But here's what I want you to remember, especially if this chapter feels raw:

**Their betrayal is not your worth.**

Let's begin the process of reclaiming what was taken, and healing in a way that brings *you* home to yourself.

---

## Betrayal Isn't Always Obvious

When we hear the word *betrayal*, we often think of cheating. And yes, infidelity is a devastating breach of trust. But betrayal comes in many forms, and they all matter:

- Promises broken again and again

- GaslIghting or emotional manipulation

- Lying by omission or deception

- Cold emotional withdrawal during your moments of need

- Repeated minimisation of your pain

- Violating your emotional or physical boundaries

If someone consistently made you feel unsafe, small, or invisible in the very space where you were most vulnerable, **that is betrayal**.

And it is valid to grieve it.

Even if they didn't "mean to." Even if they said sorry. Even if you still love them.

---

## Betrayal Creates Trauma

Let's talk about why this hurts so much.

Betrayal doesn't just break your heart. It disrupts your *sense of reality*.

You start doubting yourself:

- *Did I miss the signs?*

- *Why didn't I listen to my gut?*

- *Am I just not good enough to be chosen, protected, or told the truth?*

This is betrayal trauma. It creates a rupture in your nervous system. Suddenly, the person who once felt like home now feels like danger. And your brain scrambles to make sense of the contradiction.

This is why even *after* the breakup, you might feel anxious, hypervigilant, emotionally numb, or wildly reactive. You're not crazy. You're trying to restore a shattered sense of safety.

And that restoration starts within you.

---

## Rebuilding Your Sense of Safety

After betrayal, safety doesn't come from controlling the next person or avoiding relationships forever.

**It comes from learning to trust yourself again.**

That might feel impossible right now. You may think, *"But I let this happen. I trusted the wrong person. I ignored the signs."*

Here's a truth you need to hear:

You didn't fail. You were *open*. You were *believing*. You were *loving*.

Don't punish your heart for being generous.

Now, rebuilding safety looks like this:

- Listening to your gut, even when it's inconvenient

- Validating your feelings, even when others don't

- Creating emotional boundaries and keeping them

- Choosing people who honour your vulnerability

- Saying no when something doesn't feel right

Your nervous system heals when you stop abandoning yourself to keep someone else.

---

## Letting Go Without Needing Revenge or Apology

One of the hardest parts of betrayal is the lack of justice. You might never get the apology. They may never take responsibility. They might even twist the story to protect themselves.

And that feels... *infuriating*.

It's normal to want them to hurt the way you hurt. To want them to *see* what they did. To want closure or justice or redemption.

But here's the hard truth:

**Waiting for them to make it right keeps you tied to them.**

And you, love, deserve to be *free*.

Letting go isn't about excusing what they did. It's about choosing your peace over their punishment.

It's about saying:

> "You don't have to understand how much you hurt me. I understand. And I choose to heal anyway."

That's not weakness. That's power.

---

## Story: The Apology That Never Came

Let me tell you about *Lena*. Her partner had cheated, lied, and then blamed *her* for being "too suspicious." After they broke up, he moved on quickly, posting happy photos online like nothing had happened.

Lena was devastated. But more than that, she was *furious*. She waited for months for an apology. Acknowledgment. *Something.*

It never came.

She wrote long, unsent messages. She cried over closure she never got. And then, one day, in therapy, she said something that changed everything:

> "Maybe I don't need him to say sorry.
> Maybe I just need to believe myself."

That day, Lena burned the last letter she wrote him. She told her story, truthfully, to herself. And then she chose to stop chasing validation.

She didn't forgive him that day. But she started forgiving herself.

And that was the beginning of her freedom.

---

## Forgiveness Is for *Your* Freedom

Let's be clear: forgiveness isn't about pretending it didn't hurt. It's not about letting them off the hook. It's not about becoming best friends or sending blessings.

Forgiveness is:

- Choosing to stop carrying the pain they left you with

- Releasing the anger that's burning *you*

- Saying, *"I deserve peace, even if they don't deserve pardon"*

You can forgive and still never speak to them again.
You can forgive and still set strong boundaries.
You can forgive and still remember what happened.

Forgiveness doesn't mean forgetting.

It means you're no longer letting the betrayal define your future.

---

## Takeaways to Ground You

Let these truths sink deep:

- **Their actions are not your worth.** What they did says everything about them, not you.

- **Betrayal teaches you boundaries.** It clarifies what you will never tolerate again.

- **Forgiveness is for your freedom.** You don't have to carry this pain forever.

You may still feel raw. That's okay. You are allowed to be in process.

But every time you choose yourself over the story they wrote, you reclaim a piece of your power.

And piece by piece, you're becoming whole again.

---

## Looking Ahead...

In the next chapter, we'll talk about *loneliness*, that aching silence that follows a breakup, and how to move through it without feeling like you're disappearing. You'll learn to turn solitude into sanctuary, and remember that *you* are enough, even on the quietest nights.

Keep going. You're doing the sacred work of healing what someone else broke. And you are doing it beautifully.

# Chapter 8: Navigating Loneliness and Emptiness

It's not always the big moments that hurt the most after a breakup.

Sometimes, it's the quiet.

The silence where their good morning texts used to be.
The empty bed.
The dinners for one.
The notifications that never come.

Loneliness isn't just about missing someone's presence, it's about feeling like *you've been erased* from the life you once shared. Like you've stepped out of a world you helped build… and now you're floating in the space between what was and what's next.

It can feel like you're unmoored. Untethered. And sometimes, it's not just about losing *them*, it's about losing the version of *you* that existed when you were with them.

This chapter is for that version of you, the one trying to find yourself in the quiet.

Let's talk about why loneliness feels so heavy, and how, slowly but surely, it can become something healing instead of haunting.

## Coping With the Silence

One of the hardest adjustments after a breakup is the sheer *quiet*.

There's no one to check in with. No daily rhythm of connection. No casual conversations or shared routines. The absence is deafening, and it shows up everywhere:

- Reaching for your phone, forgetting there's no message coming

- Walking through your home and feeling the echo of them in every room

- Watching a show you both used to love, and suddenly crying without warning

- Having good news and not knowing who to share it with

That silence? It's not just inconvenient. It's *grieving made visible*.

Because when someone exits your life, they leave more than a physical void, they leave emotional space behind. And without conscious support, that space quickly fills with self-doubt, fear, and aching loneliness.

But here's the truth: **you are not meant to fill that space with their memory. You're meant to fill it with yourself.**

---

## Why Being Alone Can Feel Like Identity Loss

When we're in a relationship, especially a long or intense one, we don't just share time with someone. We build *identity* together.

- You become "us" instead of just "me."

- Your choices are often mutual.

- Your habits form around their rhythms.

- Your joy is often mirrored through their validation.

So when the relationship ends, it's not just the person who's gone, it's the version of *you* who existed with them.

You may wonder:

- *Who am I without them?*

- *What do I like doing on my own?*

- *Do I even know how to be single anymore?*

It's okay if those questions feel terrifying at first. They're not signs that you've lost yourself, they're signs that you're *on the verge of rediscovering yourself*.

You're not empty.

You're becoming.

---

## You Are Not Alone, You're in Transition

Loneliness tells you: *You've been abandoned.*

But the truth is: **You're in transition.**

And transitions feel like loss because they strip away what's familiar, even if what was familiar wasn't always good for you.

What you're going through isn't a sentence. It's a season.

It's the awkward middle part of your story, the in-between chapter where things don't feel clear yet, where the people you love feel far away, where your own voice still sounds unfamiliar.

But every person you admire has lived through this chapter too. The silence. The stretch. The rediscovery.

And every single one of them made it through.

So will you.

---

## Reframing Solitude as Sanctuary

Here's a radical thought:

**What if being alone didn't mean something's wrong? What if it's sacred?**

Solitude is not the same as loneliness.

Loneliness is the ache of absence.
 Solitude is the embrace of presence, with *yourself*.

Yes, there's grief. But there's also space now. Space to:

- Read a book without interruption

- Sleep diagonally across the bed

- Cry without hiding

- Dance in the kitchen at 2 AM

- Listen to your own needs and voice again

Solitude becomes a sanctuary when you stop trying to escape it, and start listening to what it has to teach you.

It tells you:

> "You are enough, just as you are. You do not need someone else to complete you. Your company is worthy and healing."

It might not feel like that today. But little by little, if you stay present, solitude becomes not your punishment, but your superpower.

---

## Story: The First Solo Dinner

Let me introduce you to *Erika*.

After ending a five-year relationship, she felt completely untethered. Every weekend felt like a minefield of loneliness. She dreaded Sunday evenings the most, that sinking feeling of *no one is thinking of me right now*.

One night, she did something radical: she took herself out to dinner.

Alone.

At first, she felt exposed. Everyone seemed to be laughing in pairs. She felt like a spotlight was on her table-for-one. But as the night went on, something shifted.

She started observing. Savoring. Breathing.

She read a chapter of a book. Ordered dessert. Walked home under the stars.

Later, she wrote in her journal: *"Tonight didn't make me miss him less. But for the first time in weeks, I didn't feel like I was disappearing."*

That's the magic of solitude. It returns you to *you*.

---

## You Are More Than Your Relationship Status

We live in a world that often treats singlehood like a waiting room, something to rush through on your way to the "real" life of partnership.

But your life *right now* is just as real. Just as valid. Just as beautiful.

You are not a fraction waiting to be completed.

You are whole. Even here. Even in the ache.

Your relationship status does not define your worth. Your ability to love yourself, to choose healing, to stay present in this messy in-between, *that* is what defines your strength.

---

## Takeaways to Ground You

Hold these truths close today:

- **You are not alone, you're in transition.** This is a season, not a sentence.

- **You are more than your relationship status.** You are worthy now, not just when partnered.

- **Solitude can become your superpower.** Make space, and you'll find yourself again.

So tonight, if the silence feels too loud, light a candle. Play your favourite song. Wrap yourself in a blanket and remind your heart:

> "I'm still here. And I'm learning how to love being with me."

---

## Looking Ahead…

In the next chapter, we'll explore what it means to talk about your breakup with others, and how to protect your peace while still receiving the support you need. You'll learn how to set boundaries, navigate mutual friendships, and ask for help without feeling like a burden.

You're doing the hard work of coming home to yourself.

And that, my friend, is something to be proud of.

# Chapter 9: How to Talk to Others About the Breakup

One of the hardest parts of a breakup isn't just what happens *between you and your ex*, it's what happens in the *ripple effect*.

Suddenly, you're fielding texts from friends: *"Are you okay?"*
Family members ask: *"What happened?"*
Your co-worker comments: *"I saw you two on Instagram just last month..."*
You run into mutual friends who give you that wide-eyed look, part pity, part curiosity.

And if you're anything like most people post-breakup, you're exhausted by it.

You're hurting. You're confused. And now you have to *perform* your heartbreak in conversations you may not feel ready to have.

So let's talk about how to navigate this emotional landmine with grace, setting boundaries, choosing safe people, and protecting your healing without feeling rude, guilty, or exposed.

---

## You Don't Owe Anyone Your Story

Let's start with the most important truth in this chapter:

**You are not obligated to explain your heartbreak to anyone.**

Not even to people who mean well.

Not even to the ones who ask kindly.

Not even to those who "just want to understand."

Your healing is *not* a public process. It's personal. And sacred. And it deserves to be protected, especially when you're still tender and sorting through your own feelings.

You get to choose:

- Who gets access to your heart

- How much you share

- When (or *if*) you talk about it

And saying, *"I'm not ready to talk about that yet,"* is not rude, it's self-respect.

---

## Dealing With Friends, Family, and Mutual Connections

Each group of people in your life may require a different kind of conversation, and that's okay.

### ☐ Your Inner Circle (Safe Support)

These are your go-to people. The ones who love you without needing the full explanation. The ones who say things like, *"You don't need to talk, I'm just here,"* or *"Whatever you need, I've got you."*

With them, it's safe to be raw. Unfiltered. Honest.

You don't need a script, just presence.

These are the people to lean on when your chest aches at 2 AM. The ones who let you be messy. Keep them close.

### ☐ Mutual Friends

Mutual friends can be tricky. Some will navigate the shift with grace. Others might try to stay "neutral" in a way that feels invalidating. And some may unintentionally (or intentionally) make things worse by gossiping, taking sides, or sharing details without consent.

Here's what helps:

- **Set expectations early**:
  *"I'd appreciate if we could avoid conversations about them, I'm focusing on my healing."*

- **Limit access if needed**:
  You don't have to stay close just because you once shared a social circle. Create space if you need it.

- **Protect your peace**:
  If someone constantly brings up your ex, makes you question your choices, or shares their own opinions on your breakup, they're not your support system. They're a distraction from healing.

### 👪 Family Members

Family often means well... but they don't always get it.

Your aunt may ask intrusive questions. Your dad might not know what to say at all. Your siblings might joke about it to lighten the mood, but it stings.

Here's the rule: **You get to teach people how to support you.**

Try language like:

- "Thanks for checking in. I'm working through it, but I'd rather not get into the details right now."

- "I appreciate your concern, but I'm still figuring things out, I'll share more when I'm ready."

- "I know you have advice, but what I need most is just space and love right now."

---

## Setting Boundaries Around Conversations

Boundaries are not walls, they're filters.

They keep the helpful energy in, and the harmful energy out.

Post-breakup, your emotional boundaries are like healing skin, delicate, easily irritated, vulnerable to infection. Which is why it's so important to decide:

- **What kinds of conversations help you feel supported?**

- **What kinds leave you feeling drained, judged, or triggered?**

- **Who feels emotionally safe? Who doesn't?**

And most importantly:

- **What do *you* need to feel protected right now?**

Some days you might want to talk. Other days you may need silence. Let it vary. Let it flow. And remind yourself: *It's okay to change your mind.*

---

## Asking for Support (Without Over-Sharing)

You deserve support. But support doesn't have to mean telling everyone everything.

You can be honest *and* private. You can share your emotions without every detail.

Here's a simple formula that helps:

> **State what's happening → Name what**
>
> **you need → Offer a boundary**

Example:

> "The breakup's been really painful. Right now, I'm focusing on healing. I'd love your support, but I'd rather not rehash the details."

Or:

> "I'm doing okay overall, but it still hits hard sometimes. It helps just knowing you're here. I'll reach out if I want to talk more."

Supportive people will respect that. The ones who don't? That's information.

---

## Story: When Her Friend Meant Well... But Hurt

Let me tell you about *Jessica*. After her breakup, she confided in a friend she'd known for years. The friend listened, but then started offering daily advice, gossiping about the ex, and even suggesting Jessica "just hook up with someone new to get over it."

Jessica began feeling worse after every conversation.

Eventually, she realised: *Just because someone is available doesn't mean they're helpful.*

So she had the hard conversation. She said, "I love you, but right now I need support that feels calming, not chaotic. Let's take a pause on talking about my breakup for now."

It shifted everything.

Jessica found support elsewhere, in a therapist, in journaling, in friends who *listened without fixing*. And she began healing in a way that felt *safe*.

Sometimes, loving yourself means re-evaluating who gets access to your pain.

## You Don't Need to Perform Your Healing

You don't need to look strong for anyone.
You don't need to explain your choices.
You don't need to justify your boundaries.

Healing is not a performance. It's a process.

And you get to honour it in whatever way feels true to *you*, even if that means fewer updates, more silence, and slower conversations.

## Takeaways to Ground You

Here's what I want you to carry forward:

- **Your healing doesn't need to be explained to everyone.** You can be private and still be powerful.

- **Safe circles matter during heartbreak.** Protect your peace by choosing the right people.

- **You are allowed to set boundaries around your pain.** Not everyone deserves access to your heart's most tender places.

Let your story be yours, not public property.

Let your truth be held, not dissected.

Let your voice be the one you listen to most.

---

## Looking Ahead...

In the next chapter, we'll talk about something many of us hold onto for too long: *the fantasy of "The One."* We'll gently unravel soulmate myths, explore the difference between fantasy and reality, and help you shift toward love that's rooted in truth, not longing.

You're doing the sacred work of protecting your energy. That's not selfish, it's healing.

# Chapter 10: Releasing the Fantasy of "The One"

There's a particular kind of heartbreak that hits differently.

It's not just the loss of a person.
 It's the loss of a *story*.

The story where you thought they were your forever.
 The one where you believed, *"This is it, I've found my person."*
 The fairytale you built in your mind, where it all works out because It's meant to.

And when it ends, it doesn't just hurt, it *shatters everything you believed about love.*

You're left wondering:

*Did I lose my soulmate?*
 *What if they were "The One" and I'll never find that again?*
 *How do I move on from someone I was sure I was meant to be with?*

These are real questions. And you're not foolish for asking them, you're human. But it's time to gently, lovingly, dismantle the myth that keeps so many of us stuck.

It's time to talk about *"The One."*

---

## The Soulmate Myth We've Been Sold

From childhood, we're fed stories of destiny and perfect matches.
 The one magical person who will make us feel whole.
 The lightning-bolt love that "just makes sense."
 The one who will never leave, never hurt us, and never stop choosing us.

It's beautiful. It's romantic.
 And… it's also deeply misleading.

Here's the truth: **Love is not a one-shot deal.**

There is no singular, predestined person who holds the key to your only chance at happiness. There is no cosmic punishment for losing "The One."

Instead, there are *many people you are capable of loving deeply and meaningfully,* in different ways, in different seasons of your life.

Some will come to teach you.
 Some will come to grow you.
 Some will come to break you open in painful, profound ways.

And some will come to stay, not because of fate, but because of mutual choice, conscious effort, and emotional compatibility.

---

## The End of One Love Doesn't Mean the End of Love

I know it might *feel* like you've lost your one shot.
 Like no one else will ever feel as right.
 Like no connection could possibly match the depth, intensity, or comfort of what you had.

But that's not truth. That's grief talking.
 That's the *myth of scarcity*.

The belief that love is rare. That it only comes once. That if it ends, you're forever marked by that loss.

But here's what's real:

- **Love doesn't only visit once in a lifetime.**

- **The next love can be just as deep, and possibly more aligned.**

- **You haven't missed your window. You're becoming someone even more ready for what's next.**

The love you had was real.

But so is the love still ahead of you.

---

## The Many Loves We're Meant to Meet

Throughout our lives, we meet different kinds of love:

- **The First Love**: Often intoxicating, often formative. It teaches us the thrill of romantic possibility.

- **The Lesson Love**: Intense, consuming, and usually painful. It shows us our patterns, our wounds, and what still needs healing.

- **The Companion Love**: Quiet, steady, rooted in friendship. It shows us that love doesn't always have to burn to feel warm.

- **The Conscious Love**: Mature, intentional, aligned. It doesn't just happen, it's chosen, co-created, and built on mutual growth.

Each of these loves serves a purpose. None are wasted. None are proof that you've failed. Even the ones that hurt.

Sometimes, *the point* of a relationship isn't that it lasts forever.

Sometimes, the point is that it wakes you up. Teaches you. Breaks your heart just enough to rebuild it stronger.

---

## Choosing Conscious Love Over Fantasy

Fantasy love says:

- "They complete me."

- "It shouldn't be this hard."

- "If it's meant to be, it will be."

- "Real love just clicks."

But conscious love says:

- "I am whole on my own, and I choose to share that with someone."

- "Every relationship requires growth, honesty, and effort."

- "We're not perfect, but we're committed."

- "Love isn't found, it's *built*."

Fantasy love is built on infatuation, chemistry, and projection.
Conscious love is built on trust, communication, shared values, and self-awareness.

Fantasy feels magical… until it fails to live up to the ideal.
Conscious love feels *real*. Sometimes challenging. But deeply fulfilling.

Letting go of the fantasy doesn't mean giving up on romance. It means choosing the kind of love that can actually *last*.

---

## Story: The Soulmate She Had to Leave

Let me tell you about *Aria*. She believed she had found her soulmate, someone she had been in love with since college. They had history, passion, inside jokes. Everyone said they were "meant to be."

But behind the scenes, Aria was constantly anxious. Her needs went unmet. The relationship was hot and cold. And despite the bond, she never felt fully safe or chosen.

Still, she stayed. Because how do you walk away from "The One"?

Eventually, after another round of betrayal, Aria left.

It was one of the hardest decisions of her life. She felt like she was leaving her destiny behind. But over time, she began to see the truth: it wasn't destiny, it was emotional attachment wrapped in idealisation.

Years later, she met someone else. Very different. Kinder. Calmer. No fireworks, but deep safety. Mutual respect. Steady love.

Now, she says, *"I thought I lost my soulmate. But what I actually did was create space for real love."*

---

## Real Love Starts With Reality

Real love sees the messy parts.
 Real love hears your needs and responds with care.
 Real love feels like being held, not just in arms, but emotionally, spiritually, and consistently.

You don't have to chase the fantasy.

You don't have to wait for a "perfect" person who magically reads your mind, never triggers your wounds, and completes you like a puzzle piece.

You get to choose someone who grows with you.

And until then?

You get to grow with *yourself*, the only true "One" who will be with you from your first breath to your last.

---

## Takeaways to Ground You

Let's anchor into truth:

- **The end of one love doesn't mean the end of love.** Love is abundant, not limited to one chance.

- **Growth means letting go of idealisation.** Real healing starts when we see clearly.

- **Real love starts with reality.** Not fantasy. Not fate. But conscious, mutual effort.

You didn't lose "The One."

You're releasing the illusion, so that real love can find you.

And in the meantime, you are already whole. Already worthy. Already enough.

## Looking Ahead...

In the next chapter, we begin *Part III: Rebuilding You.* We'll explore how to reclaim your identity after a breakup, rediscover who you are without them, and start writing the next beautiful chapter of your life, on your own terms.

You've made it through the hardest emotional terrain. Now, the light starts coming back in.

Ready?

# Chapter 11: Reclaiming Your Identity

At some point after a breakup, usually once the tears slow down, the panic quiets, and the daily ache begins to soften, a new question starts to rise:

*Who am I now?*

It can feel jarring. Like waking up in a life that doesn't fully feel like yours anymore. You're still here… but you're not quite *you*. Not the version of you who was in that relationship. Not yet the version of you who's healed.

You're in the in-between.

And this space? It's where identity is re-formed. Not by accident, but by *intention*.

You don't just return to who you were before the relationship. You get to become someone stronger, wiser, deeper, someone you *choose* to be, instead of someone you unconsciously adapted into.

This is your becoming.

---

## Rediscovering Who You Were Before

Start here: **You existed before them.**

Before the "we," there was *you*, in your full complexity and worth.

You had quirks, dreams, rituals, friendships. You had a voice, a rhythm, a centre of gravity that was all your own.

And maybe, during the relationship, parts of that slipped away.

It happens to the best of us.

We compromise. We shift. We accommodate. We fall in love and sometimes, without realising it, we start shrinking or reshaping ourselves to fit into a shared container.

We forget the little things:

- The music we loved

- The way we dressed when no one was watching

- The hobbies we stopped doing

- The alone time we used to cherish

- The things we believed before someone else's voice got louder than our own

The beautiful part? **That version of you didn't disappear, she's just been waiting.**

Waiting for the space to return. Waiting to be remembered. Waiting for you to choose her again.

---

## Who You Are Now, Post-Breakup

Here's the truth most people skip: **You're not the same person you were before the relationship, and you're not supposed to be.**

You've lived through love. Through loss. Through growth. Through grief.

And that changes you.

But not in a bad way.

Now, you're someone who:

- Has seen what doesn't work

- Knows more about your needs and boundaries

- Understands what love *isn't*

- Has emotional tools you didn't have before

- Can start again with more wisdom, more self-awareness, more self-respect

So don't just reach backwards to "who you used to be." Reach *inward* to who you're becoming now.

Ask:

- *What did I lose that I want to reclaim?*

- *What did I outgrow that I can release?*

- *What new values, goals, or dreams are emerging in me now?*

Your identity doesn't have to be rebuilt on grief. It can be built on truth.

---

## Creating a New Version of Self

This chapter of your life is not a return to "normal." It's a reinvention, and that's powerful.

Reinvention doesn't mean pretending the past didn't happen. It means using the experience to create a *more aligned, more grounded, more intentional* version of yourself.

Here are a few ways to begin:

### ✦ Reclaim Your Time

Re-evaluate how you spend your days now that you're not orbiting someone else's schedule, moods, or priorities.

- What do *you* want to do with your evenings?

- What morning routine nourishes *you*?

- Where have you been saying yes when you meant no?

Time is your currency, spend it on your own joy.

### ✦ Revisit Your Joy

What used to light you up? What did you let go of while trying to make the relationship work?

Start small:

- Rewatch your favourite childhood movie

- Revisit a hobby you abandoned

- Create a playlist that makes you feel alive

Joy is often the doorway back to identity.

### ✨ Redefine What You Want

You're no longer making decisions based on what's good for "us."

This is about *you*.

- What kind of future do you want?

- What kind of partner *actually* aligns with your values and vision now?

- What kind of life are you building, with or without a relationship?

This is your clean slate. You don't have to carry forward any version of yourself that doesn't feel true.

---

## Story: The Woman Who Forgot Herself

Let me tell you about *Samantha*. She had been in a long-term relationship with someone who, over time, became subtly controlling. He never outright told her to stop doing things, but she noticed she stopped wearing certain clothes, stopped going to dance class, stopped sharing opinions he might challenge.

After the breakup, she didn't cry much. What she felt instead was… *empty.*

"I don't even know what I like anymore," she said. "I've spent so long adapting to him that I forgot who I am."

But slowly, she started to piece it back together.

She bought herself a bike. She got a tattoo she'd wanted for years but he didn't approve of. She started travelling solo. She even dyed her hair bright red, just because.

She looked in the mirror one day and whispered: *"Oh. There I am."*

That's what reclaiming your identity looks like. Not a dramatic overhaul. But small, true choices that feel like *you*.

---

## Breakups Break Illusions, Not Your Identity

It's easy to think that the relationship *defined you*. That your identity was built around being "the girlfriend," "the wife," "the partner."

But what the breakup actually did was **break the illusion that you had to be anything other than yourself.**

You haven't lost who you are, you're just seeing yourself more clearly now.

And that clarity?

It's the foundation of everything you're about to become.

---

## You Get to Reinvent Yourself With Intention

This next chapter isn't about proving anything. It's not about "glowing up" to show your ex what they lost. It's not about becoming someone so desirable that you never get left again.

It's about becoming someone *you* love. Someone you wake up proud of. Someone who feels like home to herself.

You get to reinvent:

- How you show up in relationships

- How you speak to yourself

- What you allow and what you no longer tolerate

- What kind of life you're building, with no apologies

This is the season where you stop abandoning yourself.

This is the season where you choose *you*.

---

## Takeaways to Ground You

Let's anchor these truths in your heart:

- **You are whole on your own.** You don't need a relationship to define or complete you.

- **Breakups break illusions, not your identity.** You are still *you*, maybe even more so.

- **You get to reinvent yourself with intention.** This isn't the end, it's a redesign.

So if you feel a little lost right now, take heart.

You're not lost, you're *becoming*.

And the person you're becoming? She's already inside you.

You're just coming home to her now.

---

## Looking Ahead...

In the next chapter, we'll talk about *how to rebuild your self-esteem and confidence* after a breakup, especially if your sense of worth took a hit. You'll learn how to quiet the inner critic, strengthen your inner voice, and walk taller in your truth again.

You are already growing.

Let's keep going.

# Chapter 12: Boosting Self-Esteem and Confidence

One of the quietest casualties of a breakup is your **self-esteem**.

You may not even realise how much it's been chipped away, until you find yourself second-guessing your worth, questioning your decisions, or looking in the mirror and wondering, *"What happened to me?"*

Breakups can shake the core of who we are, not just emotionally, but internally. Especially if the relationship left you feeling unseen, dismissed, criticised, betrayed, or not chosen.

Whether the damage was subtle or sharp, the message you may have internalised is this:

*I wasn't enough.*

And nothing could be further from the truth.

This chapter is your invitation to unlearn those lies. To turn down the volume on your inner critic. To build back belief in yourself, not in one dramatic leap, but in small, quiet, powerful ways.

Because confidence isn't something you "get back."

It's something you *build*, one choice, one moment, one thought at a time.

---

## Undoing the Erosion of Self-Worth

Let's name what might have eroded your self-esteem in the relationship or during the breakup:

- Repeated criticism or emotional withdrawal

- Being blamed for issues you didn't create

- Feeling like your needs were "too much"

- Being cheated on, ghosted, or dismissed

- Trying hard to "fix it" and still being left

- Losing your sense of identity in the relationship

All of these experiences send subtle, or not-so-subtle, messages to your nervous system:

- *I'm not lovable as I am.*

- *My voice doesn't matter.*

- *No matter what I do, I'm not enough.*

Over time, these messages become beliefs. Beliefs that feel like *truth*.

But they're not truths, they're wounds. And wounds, when tended to, can heal.

---

## Inner Critic vs Inner Ally

We all have an inner voice. After a breakup, that voice can turn harsh.

- *"Why did I let this happen?"*

- *"I should've seen the red flags."*

- *"I'm too broken."*

- *"Who would want me now?"*

This is your **inner critic**, a voice formed by past pain, trauma, cultural conditioning, and unmet emotional needs.

But you also have another voice, even if it's quiet right now.

That's your **inner ally**.

She's the one who says:

- *"You did your best."*

- *"You're allowed to grow and change."*

- *"You're still worthy."*

- *"This doesn't define you."*

The shift toward self-esteem begins when you *consciously choose* to listen to your inner ally more than your inner critic.

It's not about silencing the critic completely, it's about *not letting her drive the car anymore*.

---

## Confidence Is a Daily Practice, Not a Feeling

We often think of confidence as something we're either born with or "get" once we've achieved something big. But in reality:

> **Confidence is built by consistently showing up for yourself, even when you feel scared, unsure, or messy.**

Confidence sounds like:

- Saying no when it's hard

- Speaking kindly to yourself

- Trying something new without perfection

- Setting a boundary and honouring it

- Taking care of your body, your space, your needs

- Asking for help when you need it

You don't wait for confidence to arrive before you act.

You act, and that's how confidence is born.

It's a muscle.

And every time you choose yourself, you strengthen it.

---

## Small Wins That Rebuild Belief

You don't need a full makeover, a dream job, or a new relationship to feel confident again.

What you need are *small wins* that remind you: *"I'm capable. I matter. I can trust myself."*

Try these simple confidence builders:

### ✅ Micro-Actions

- Make your bed each morning, a small act of self-respect

- Cook a nourishing meal for yourself

- Take a walk and listen to a podcast that inspires you

- Send a kind text to a friend or yourself

- Wear something that makes *you* feel good

- Practice saying "no", even to small things

Each action says, *"I care about me."*

And every time you care for yourself, your self-worth recalibrates.

### 📝 "I Am" Journal Prompt

Each day for 7 days, write 3 sentences starting with "I am…"

They can be true today or things you're growing into:

- *I am resilient.*

- *I am learning to love myself.*

- *I am allowed to take up space.*

Let your subconscious begin to meet you there.

---

## Story: Starting Stronger, Not Over

Meet *Nina*. After a painful breakup where she was cheated on, Nina felt completely gutted. Her confidence disappeared. She said, *"I feel like I'm starting from zero."*

But slowly, she began choosing herself again.

She started therapy. She stopped checking his social media. She joined a weekly dance class she'd been too scared to try. She stopped apologising for her emotions.

One day, she said something powerful in session:

"I'm not starting over. I'm starting stronger."

Because she wasn't who she was before the breakup, she was *better*.

More self-aware. More grounded. More intentional.

That's the truth for you, too.

You're not back at the beginning.

You're on new ground, and this time, you're building with *you* in mind.

---

## You Are Worthy of Love and Respect

Let me say it again:

**You are worthy.**

Not because you were chosen.
 Not because someone else validates you.
 Not because you're perfect, or healed, or happy all the time.

You are worthy *because you are human*.

You're allowed to be soft and strong.
 Tender and powerful.
 Healing and still whole.

Your confidence doesn't need to be loud. It just needs to be *yours*.

---

## Takeaways to Ground You

Let these truths settle into your heart:

- **You are worthy of love and respect, now, not later.**

- **Confidence is a daily practice, not a personality trait.**

- **You're not starting over, you're starting stronger.**

This is the part of your journey where you stop asking for permission and start reclaiming your own voice.

Step by step, you're becoming someone you can rely on.

Someone you *trust*.

And that's the kind of confidence no one can take away.

---

## Looking Ahead...

In the next chapter, we'll take this newfound confidence and shift your *mindset* around love itself. You'll learn to move from scarcity thinking (*"What if I never find love again?"*) to abundance thinking (*"I trust that love will find me when I'm ready"*).

Your relationship with yourself is strengthening. Now we'll shape how you view love, not with fear, but with clarity and choice.

You're doing beautifully. Let's keep going.

# Chapter 13: Resetting Your Mindset Around Love

There's a quiet fear that creeps in after a breakup, especially one that felt serious, long-term, or deeply meaningful.

It whispers:

*What if I never find that kind of love again?*
*What if I missed my chance?*
*What if that was my person?*
*What if I'm too old / too late / too damaged to find love again?*

This fear isn't just about loss. It's about **lack**, the belief that love is limited, and that you've somehow fallen behind or been left out.

It's what we call **scarcity mindset**, and it's one of the most painful and paralysing beliefs you can carry after a breakup.

But here's what's true:

**Love is not scarce. Love is not a race. Love is not something you have to prove you're worthy of.**

Love is abundant. Love is available. Love is *still* possible for you, and it will come, not in the same way it did before, but in a way that's wiser, safer, and better aligned with who you're becoming.

Let's reset your mindset, and open the door to a healthier, more empowered way of seeing love.

---

## Scarcity Thinking vs. Abundance Thinking

Scarcity thinking says:

- "Everyone else is in a relationship."

- "There's no one out there for me."

- "If I don't hurry, I'll end up alone."

- "That was my only real shot."

- "I need someone to choose me, so I can feel whole again."

Abundance thinking says:

- "I trust that the right person will meet me at the right time."

- "I don't have to settle just to feel wanted."

- "I am already whole, and love will only add to my life."

- "My timeline is not wrong, it's *mine*."

- "Every relationship taught me something I'll take forward."

Scarcity is rooted in fear, comparison, urgency, and pressure.

Abundance is rooted in trust, presence, self-worth, and clarity.

One creates desperation.
The other creates alignment.

---

## Love Is Not a Prize You Earn

We live in a culture that often treats romantic love like a reward. If you're beautiful enough, kind enough, accomplished enough, healed enough, *then* you'll get the relationship you want.

But this belief creates pressure. It makes you feel like you have to constantly perform or improve in order to be chosen.

Here's the truth:

**Love is not something you earn. It's something you experience, create, and *choose*, in mutual partnership with someone else.**

You don't have to be perfect to be loved. You don't have to check every box. You don't have to "heal all your wounds" before someone can love you.

You just have to be *you*, real, honest, self-aware, growing.

Love is not a gold medal. It's a human connection. It's two people choosing each other, not because they're perfect, but because they're *aligned and committed*.

---

## Shifting From "I Need Someone" to "I Choose Wisely"

After heartbreak, it's natural to crave connection. To want someone to fill the space. To want the comfort, intimacy, and reassurance that love can bring.

But when love becomes a *need* instead of a *choice*, we lose our power.

We settle. We chase. We compromise. We confuse attention with affection, chemistry with compatibility, familiarity with fate.

Let's change the internal script:

From:

> *"I need someone to choose me so I can feel okay again."*

To:

> *"I am okay as I am, and I will choose someone who reflects my growth, not my wounds."*

From:

> *"I just want someone to love me."*

To:

> *"I want to love and be loved in a way that feels safe, honest, and mutual."*

This is where your agency lives.

You don't just want love. You want *the right* love, and that means *you get to be selective.*

---

## Story: From Scarcity to Self-Trust

Meet *Alicia*. After a three-year relationship ended, she was terrified. Most of her friends were married or having kids. She was 37, and all she could think was, *"I'm behind. Everyone else has figured it out."*

So she downloaded dating apps, forced herself on awkward dates, and tried to push past the grief.

But nothing felt right.

Eventually, she paused. Took a break. Focused on healing, community, and rebuilding her own joy.

Over time, her mindset began to shift. She stopped seeing herself as "behind." She stopped treating love like a job interview.

She started saying, *"If I'm going to open my heart again, it has to feel right in my soul, not just look good on paper."*

That's when everything changed.

She met someone, slowly, organically, through a shared interest. Someone who respected her pace, matched her values, and saw her clearly.

Now she says, *"I thought I needed to be chosen. But actually, I just needed to choose me first."*

---

## There Is No Rush, You're Not Behind

Let's be honest, it can feel like love has a deadline. Especially if you're watching people get engaged, married, or post anniversary photos on Instagram every other week.

But timelines are illusions.

You're not on anyone else's clock.

You are not late. You are not falling behind. You are not "behind schedule" because you're healing, growing, or taking your time.

Love is not a linear path. It's not a race to the altar.

It's a deeply personal journey, and the love that aligns with you will never require you to abandon yourself to keep up.

---

## Love Will Come Again, But Differently and Better

You may still miss what you had. You may still long for the connection, the familiarity, the feeling of being held.

That's okay.

But the love that's coming next? It won't look like the last one.

It will be clearer.
It will be calmer.
It will feel like choice, not chase.
It will reflect the person you're becoming, not the person you were.

And that is something to look forward to.

---

## Takeaways to Ground You

Let these truths settle into your heart:

- **Your value isn't tied to someone choosing you.** You are already worthy.

- **There is no rush, you're not behind.** Your love story unfolds at your own pace.

- **Love will come again, but differently and better.** When you choose yourself, you change what you attract.

You don't need to chase love.

You just need to keep becoming someone who loves herself so deeply that anything less than truth, safety, and alignment simply doesn't fit anymore.

---

## Looking Ahead…

In the next chapter, we'll begin bringing joy back into your everyday life. We'll explore how to create happiness *before* you're "fully healed," how joy itself can be a form of healing, and how to rebuild a life that feels fun, vibrant, and beautifully your own.

You've done the deep emotional work, now it's time to let some light in.

Let's keep going. You're doing this beautifully.

# Chapter 14: Building a Joy-Filled Life Again

Somewhere along the path of heartbreak, we begin to forget what joy feels like.

The days get heavier. Your routines revolve around surviving. You might smile, sure, but it feels mechanical. Empty, even. Like you're playing a role instead of living your life.

And when someone says "do something fun," you might think: *I don't even remember what fun is anymore.*

Here's what I want to remind you:

> **You are allowed to feel joy, even in the middle of healing.**
> **You are allowed to laugh, even while grieving.**
> **You are allowed to be happy, even before you feel "fully over it."**

In fact, joy is part of the healing.

This chapter is your permission slip to *reclaim it*. Not by forcing yourself to "move on," but by slowly, gently, inviting colour back into your world. One laugh. One moment. One bold, messy, beautiful choice at a time.

---

## Reclaiming Joy, Purpose, and Fun

When your heart breaks, it often takes your sense of purpose with it. Especially if you built your identity around the relationship. The plans. The future you imagined.

So much energy goes into surviving the loss, managing the pain, and "figuring things out" that we forget joy even exists.

But joy isn't just something that *happens to you*.
It's something you can *choose* to make space for again.

And no, it doesn't have to be grand or Instagram-worthy. You don't have to take a solo trip to Bali or sign up for a silent retreat (unless that's your thing).

Joy often lives in the small, unexpected places:

- Singing in your car with the windows down

- Dancing in your kitchen at midnight

- Saying yes to an impromptu coffee with a friend

- Reading a book that makes you laugh out loud

- Creating something with your hands

- Walking barefoot in the grass

- Trying something completely new with zero expectations

These things don't erase the sadness. But they remind you: *I'm still here. And there is still beauty in being alive.*

---

## Creating New Routines and Adventures

One of the most powerful things you can do post-breakup is **create new structure around your new life**. Not as a distraction, but as a declaration:

*This is my life now. And I get to shape it.*

Start with your routines.

Ask yourself:

- What does *morning* look like now, if I'm designing it for *me*?

- What habits nourish my energy instead of depleting it?

- How can I build in small moments of pleasure into my days?

Even something as simple as making your coffee a little slower in the morning, stretching while listening to music, or lighting a candle at night just for you, these tiny acts are statements of self-love.

Now layer in adventure.

Adventure doesn't have to be big. It just has to be **new**.

- Take a class in something you've never tried

- Visit a nearby town you've never explored

- Host a dinner party with zero expectations

- Learn to cook a new cuisine

- Join a group or meetup that interests you, even if it's a little scary

New experiences shake us out of grief autopilot and awaken the part of us that remembers: *There is still so much life ahead.*

---

## Making Space for Spontaneity

In a relationship, especially one that became routine or tense, spontaneity can go out the window. So can silliness. So can the sense of *freedom* to just… do things.

So now, you get to bring that back.

Let spontaneity return, even in small ways:

- Say yes to the last-minute invitation

- Try on a bold outfit you wouldn't normally wear

- Take yourself on a "yes day" where you follow curiosity wherever it leads

- Leave room in your schedule for play, not productivity

Here's a little secret:

**Spontaneity isn't irresponsible , it's restorative.**

It's how your nervous system relearns *safety in freedom*. It's how you reclaim a sense of possibility. It's how you start to feel *alive* again, not just functional.

---

## Story: The "Joy Calendar" That Changed Everything

Let me introduce you to *Erin*.

After a long-term relationship ended, she found herself stuck in a fog. Wake up. Work. Cry. Scroll. Repeat.

One day, her therapist said, *"What if you scheduled joy the way you schedule meetings?"*

So Erin made a calendar.

She called it her *Joy Reclaiming Calendar.*

Each week, she wrote in one thing that made her feel curious, excited, playful, or even just mildly interested. Some weeks it was "paint something badly." Others it was "go to a farmer's market and buy the weirdest fruit." One week, it was "watch stand-up comedy until I laugh-snort."

Week by week, something shifted.

She wasn't waiting for happiness to magically return. She was **inviting it**, deliberately, gently, consistently.

Joy didn't erase her grief. But it reminded her she was more than it.

---

## Exercise: Your "Joy Reclaiming Calendar"

Grab a blank calendar, or just a notebook, and map out the next 30 days.

Choose one joy-oriented action per week. Start small. Think:

- Go somewhere I've never been

- Listen to a nostalgic playlist

- Watch a ridiculous comedy

- Try something creatively playful (bad art encouraged!)

- Invite someone to do something unexpected with me

- Wear something bold or silly just for fun

You don't have to *feel like it* ahead of time. You just have to *show up* for it.

Let joy meet you there.

---

## You Deserve Happiness, Even Before You're "Fully Healed"

Here's the truth many people struggle with:

**You don't have to be completely healed to be happy.**

You don't have to wait until all the sadness is gone. Until you've figured it all out. Until you no longer think of your ex. Until you're 100% confident and glowing.

You deserve moments of joy *now*.
 You deserve laughter *now*.
 You deserve pleasure, connection, and lightness *now*.

Because happiness isn't a finish line, it's a way of living alongside everything else.

Let yourself have it. You're not betraying your healing. You're expanding it.

---

## Takeaways to Ground You

Let's anchor what we've explored:

- **You deserve happiness, even before you're "fully healed."** Joy is not a reward for recovery. It's a tool for it.

- **Joy heals too.** It soothes your nervous system, opens your heart, and reminds you who you are.

- **A fulfilled life attracts aligned love.** When you live with purpose, play, and presence, you become magnetic, not because you're trying, but because you're *whole*.

You are allowed to feel good again.

You are allowed to fall back in love with your own life.

This is your moment to say yes, to joy, to adventure, to *you*.

---

## Looking Ahead...

In the next chapter, we'll shift from emotional healing to **practical space clearing**, digital, physical, and emotional. You'll learn how to declutter your world from lingering reminders, triggers, and attachments that no longer serve the future you're building.

You're stepping into a new season, and it deserves space to grow.

Let's make room for what's next.

# Chapter 15: Cleaning House –
# Digital, Physical, Emotional

You've done so much inner work, felt the pain, untangled the memories, started reclaiming your joy. Now it's time to turn outward. To look around your world, your space, your screens, your soul, and ask:

**What am I still holding onto that no longer belongs in the life I'm creating?**

Because healing isn't just about your thoughts and feelings.

It's also about your *environment*.

Every text thread you haven't deleted, every hoodie of theirs tucked in your drawer, every song that instantly brings you to tears, those are *emotional anchors*. They pull you back when you're trying to move forward.

> **Cleaning house, digitally, physically, emotionally, is not about pretending nothing happened. It's about honouring what did, while gently releasing what no longer serves your next chapter.**

This is your space. Your energy. Your future.
Let's clear some room for it.

---

## Removing Triggers and Reminders

Let's start with what's obvious, the things that *sting* when you see or touch them:

- Photos on your phone

- Old texts or email threads

- Their belongings still in your home

- Social media connections or shared playlists

- Notes, gifts, cards

- Shared calendars or journals

- That one shirt that still smells like them

It's normal to feel resistance here.

You might tell yourself:

- *"I'm not ready to delete those photos."*

- *"What if I need those texts one day?"*

- *"It's just a hoodie, it doesn't mean anything."*

But here's the truth: **Every time you see those things, your nervous system gets reactivated.** It's a small heartbreak all over again. A subtle message that says, *"You're still there."*

And you're not.

You're *here*, in your new life, doing the hard and beautiful work of becoming someone new.

Letting go of reminders doesn't erase the relationship. It creates room for *you*.

---

## Creating Healing Spaces

Once you remove the triggers, the next step is to *reclaim* your environment.

Ask yourself:

- What spaces in my home feel heavy or emotionally charged?

- What rooms, drawers, or closets have "ghosts" of the relationship?

- What could I shift, even slightly, to make things feel more *mine*?

You don't need a full renovation.

Even small changes send powerful psychological signals:

- Rearranging your furniture to shift the energy

- Buying a new bedsheet or throw pillow in a colour that makes you feel good

- Turning their old shelf into a "self-love" shelf with your favourite books, candles, affirmations, or keepsakes

- Creating a corner that's just for joy, art, music, journaling, or simply sitting in silence with tea and peace

You're saying to yourself:
**"This space is for me now. This life is for me now."**

And over time, those external cues reinforce your internal transformation.

---

## Emotional Spring Cleaning

Now, let's go a level deeper.

Beyond the digital files and physical objects, there's emotional clutter. Lingering energy. Unspoken truths. Mental loops that take up way too much space in your heart.

This is where we ask:

- What guilt am I still carrying?

- What conversations am I still rehearsing in my head?

- What hopes or fantasies am I afraid to fully let go of?

- What part of me is still waiting for closure, or a different ending?

Emotional spring cleaning isn't about "getting over it." It's about *freeing up your energy.*

You can start small:

### 📝 A Simple Letting Go Practice

1. **Write down** anything you feel ready (or almost ready) to release.

   - "The hope they'll come back."

- "The feeling that it was my fault."

- "The regret over how it ended."

- "The need to explain myself to them."

2. **Read it aloud to yourself.** Feel what comes up.

3. **Destroy it intentionally** , rip it, burn it safely, delete it.

This isn't magic. It's *symbolic action* that affirms your decision to move forward.

And your nervous system *loves* closure rituals. They help your body catch up with your mind.

---

## Story: Clearing the Closet, Clearing Her Heart

*Jasmine* had been broken up with her ex for four months, but her apartment still looked like they lived there.

Photos on the fridge. His hoodie in the laundry basket. A drawer in the bathroom still half full of his stuff.

"I kept thinking I'd deal with it later," she said. "But every time I saw his toothbrush, my chest would tighten."

One weekend, she finally decided to clear it out. She turned on music, called a friend for moral support, and went room by room.

She cried. Laughed at old memories. Grieved. But at the end of the weekend, her space felt *light*. *Hers*.

She said, *"I thought getting rid of his stuff would make me feel more alone. But it actually made me feel free."*

Sometimes, the thing you're afraid to let go of is the very thing blocking your peace.

---

## Your Environment Affects Your Emotional Energy

Ever notice how a messy kitchen or cluttered closet makes your brain feel foggy? Or how sitting in a sunlit space can change your whole mood?

That's not a coincidence. Your outer environment is often a reflection of your inner one.

And sometimes, we keep things not because we need them, but because we're scared to face what their absence means.

Here's the truth:

**Letting go is both symbolic and strategic.**

When you remove what no longer belongs, you create space for what *does*.

That might be peace.
Clarity.
A deep breath.
Or simply the ability to wake up in your own home and feel *safe and grounded*.

---

## Create Space for the New by Releasing the Old

You don't have to "erase" the past to honour your growth.
But you do need to release what holds you hostage in it.

Think of this process like preparing soil for planting.

You're not destroying the garden. You're pulling up the weeds. Clearing out debris. Making room for something beautiful to grow.

And that something… is *you*.

The next version of you. The one who isn't haunted by reminders, but supported by space. The one who makes intentional choices about what to keep, and what to lovingly let go.

This is your clearing season.
What comes next is entirely yours to create.

---

## Takeaways to Ground You

Let's bring this all together:

- **Your environment affects your emotional energy.** What surrounds you influences how you feel.

- **Letting go is both symbolic and strategic.** It helps your mind, heart, and body release what's no longer needed.

- **Create space for the new by releasing the old.** Clarity, peace, and joy need room to grow.

You deserve a space that reflects your healing.
You deserve to walk through your home and feel *safe, seen,* and *centered*.

You are not erasing the past, you are preparing for the future.

And it's going to be beautiful.

---

## Looking Ahead...

In the next chapter, we'll explore one of the most powerful tools in your healing journey: **forgiveness**. Not the "forgive and forget" kind, but the real, raw, freeing kind that allows you to let go of resentment, reclaim your power, and make peace with what happened... even if they never said sorry.

You're making space. Now we'll fill it, with peace, strength, and liberation.

# Chapter 16: Forgiving Without Forgetting

Let's be honest, few words feel more complicated after a breakup than *forgiveness*.

You might be thinking:

- *Why should I forgive someone who hurt me?*

- *Does forgiving them mean what they did was okay?*

- *What if I'm not ready? What if I never will be?*

And most of all:

*If I forgive… will I forget? Will I let my guard down? Will I lose myself again?*

Here's what I want you to know:

> **Forgiveness is not about excusing what happened. It's about choosing freedom, for *you*.**
>
> **Forgiveness is not forgetting. It's remembering *without carrying the pain*.**

**Forgiveness doesn't mean going back. It means *moving forward*, unburdened.**

This chapter isn't here to push you or preach at you. It's here to gently show you that forgiveness isn't something you do *for them*. It's a gift you give *yourself*, so you can finally breathe again.

Let's take this one honest step at a time.

---

## What Real Forgiveness Looks Like

Forgiveness isn't about denial. It's not blind. It's not pretending you weren't hurt. It's not forcing a smile and acting like everything's fine.

Real forgiveness says:

- "Yes, it happened."

- "Yes, it hurt."

- "No, it wasn't okay."

- "And I'm *still* choosing to release this pain, because it no longer belongs in my body."

It's not a one-time event. It's a process.

Sometimes it happens in layers. Sometimes you think you've forgiven, and then a memory reopens the wound. That's okay.

Forgiveness isn't linear.

It's a gradual loosening of the grip the pain has on your heart.

It's the moment you realise you haven't checked their socials in weeks. The moment their name no longer makes your chest tighten. The moment you hear their favourite song and… you just keep walking.

That's forgiveness at work. Quiet. Subtle. Powerful.

---

## Releasing Resentment for *Your* Peace

Here's the hard truth: resentment is heavy.

It may feel righteous. It may feel justified. But it's also *exhausting*.

When you carry resentment, you're still giving them power. You're still tethered to the pain. You're still stuck in the story of what happened.

But peace? Peace is yours to reclaim.

Letting go of resentment doesn't mean they get away with it.
It means *you* get to walk away free.

**Forgiveness says, "I'm not carrying this anymore. Not for another day."**

You can still have boundaries. You can still choose distance.
But inside your own heart, you get to stop being at war.

And that peace… it's not just relief. It's *healing*.

---

## You Can Forgive and Still Never Go Back

Let's make something really clear:

You can forgive someone…
   … and still block their number.
   … and still never let them back into your life.
   … and still honour your *no*.

Forgiveness is about your *emotional state*, not your relationship status.

It doesn't mean reconnection. It means **reclamation**, of your peace, your values, your energy.

You're not required to welcome someone back just because you've forgiven them. In fact, your very ability to forgive might come from having *healthy distance*.

And if they were abusive, manipulative, or toxic?

Forgiveness might look like *never seeing or speaking to them again*, while still choosing to release what they did from ruling your thoughts or stealing your joy.

---

## Story: The Forgiveness Letter That Was Never Sent

*Logan* was betrayed by someone he thought he'd marry. The breakup wasn't just painful, it was humiliating. Friends took sides. Rumours spread. He felt shattered.

For months, he carried resentment. "Why should I forgive someone who never apologised?" he asked.

But the anger was eating him alive.

His therapist suggested writing a letter, not to send, but to express.

So he did.

He poured out everything: the pain, the confusion, the loss, the rage. And then, at the very end, he wrote: *"I forgive you. Not because you deserve it, but because I deserve peace."*

He read it once, cried, and burned it.

He says it was the turning point in his healing. Not because it changed the past. But because it changed *his relationship to it.*

Sometimes forgiveness doesn't change them.
 It changes *you.*

---

## Forgiveness Is for You, Not Them

So many people think forgiveness is about the other person.

It's not.

It's about *releasing yourself* from the burden of bitterness.

It's about letting go of the fantasy that they'll make it right. That they'll understand. That they'll apologise in just the right way.

You don't need that.

You don't need them to be sorry to set yourself free.

You just need to decide: *I'm done letting this pain lead my life.*

You're not weak for forgiving. You're wise.

---

## You Can Let Go Without Losing Your Standards

Forgiveness doesn't mean you accept less.

In fact, it usually means your standards are getting higher.

Because once you release someone who hurt you, and forgive them not for their sake, but for your own, you start to realise:

- I deserve love that feels safe.

- I deserve honesty.

- I deserve respect.

- I deserve consistency.

- I deserve to *never* question my worth again.

Forgiveness clears the ground.

And now, you get to build something healthier on it.

---

## Peace > Bitterness

Bitterness is seductive. It tells you you're strong.
Protected. Guarded.

But it also keeps your heart closed.

And while it's okay to be cautious, your heart *wants* to
stay open.
 Not for them. For *you*.

Because love will come again.

And this time, it will be chosen *from peace, not panic*.
From clarity, not confusion. From wholeness, not
wounds.

Forgiveness is the bridge from heartbreak to hope.

Cross it when you're ready.

You don't have to rush.

But when you do, you'll feel the lightness of carrying
only what's yours, not what they left behind.

---

## Takeaways to Ground You

Let's let these truths sink in:

- **Forgiveness is for you, not them.** It's a radical act of self-liberation.

- **You can let go without losing your standards.** Releasing the pain raises the bar.

- **Peace > bitterness.** Because peace is where your power lives.

You are not weak for forgiving. You are *brave*.
 You are not erasing the past. You're reclaiming your future.

And you are absolutely allowed to move forward with love, clarity, and grace.

---

## Looking Ahead...

In the next chapter, we'll explore something beautiful: **how to recognise the signs you're truly healing.** From subtle emotional shifts to stronger boundaries and self-trust, we'll reflect on the quiet progress you've made, even if it doesn't feel dramatic.

Because healing doesn't always announce itself.
Sometimes, it just *feels like coming home* to yourself.

# Chapter 17: How to Know You're Healing

Healing doesn't always come with fireworks.

Sometimes, it comes in whispers.

Not in the grand milestones, but in the *ordinary moments* when something that used to sting... doesn't. When a thought crosses your mind and instead of breaking you, it just *passes through*.

Often, we're so focused on what's *still hurting*, we forget to notice what's no longer bleeding.

That's what this chapter is here for.

To help you pause. Breathe. And see that healing isn't about being "over it" all at once, it's about learning to live with softness, strength, and increasing lightness again.

Let's explore the subtle, powerful signs that you are, whether you realise it or not, healing.

---

## Sign #1: You're Less Triggered by Their Name, Face, or Memory

One of the first, and most unexpected, signs of healing is emotional *neutrality*.

That name that once made your heart race? Now it barely registers.
 That photo you used to cry over? Now it feels... distant.
 That song that made you ache? Now you sing along without pain.

This isn't numbness. This is *integration.*

You've metabolised the memory. You've stopped assigning it emotional charge. It's not erased, it just no longer defines you.

You may not even notice it happening at first. But one day, you'll catch yourself scrolling past an old memory and think, *Huh. That didn't hurt this time.*

That's healing.

---

## Sign #2: You're Not Obsessively Replaying the Story

In the beginning, your mind is like a broken record:

- *Why did they do that?*

- *What if I had said this instead?*

- *Were they thinking of me?*

- *Was it even real?*

It's exhausting. And normal.

But healing shows up when the story no longer runs your thoughts.

It starts with longer stretches of silence in your mind. With less analysis. Fewer "what ifs." More *presence*.

You begin to live in *now*, not *then*.

You realise that the story, while important, doesn't deserve a front-row seat anymore. And slowly, it moves to the back of the theatre, until it's just a dim figure in the distance.

---

## Sign #3: You're Taking Care of Yourself Without It Feeling Like a Struggle

At first, even basic self-care can feel hard. Eating well. Sleeping. Brushing your hair. Making plans. All of it feels like climbing uphill.

But healing often sneaks in through **consistency**.

You start making your bed again.
You prep your meals with care.
You go on a walk not because you *have* to, but

because it feels good.
You catch your reflection and smile, *actually smile*, without forcing it.

Self-respect returns through tiny rituals of care.

You're not punishing yourself for the breakup anymore. You're *nurturing* yourself back to life.

---

## Sign #4: You're Trusting Yourself Again

Heartbreak shakes our trust, especially in ourselves.

You may have thought:

- *How did I not see it coming?*

- *Why did I ignore the red flags?*

- *Can I even trust myself to love again?*

But here's what healing looks like:

- You start listening to your intuition.

- You set a boundary and stick to it.

- You reflect on the past without shaming yourself, just learning.

- You feel less afraid of your own heart.

You realise that mistakes don't make you unworthy.
That your judgment wasn't broken, it was just learning.

And now? You're wiser. Sharper. More grounded.
You trust yourself to *know* better and *do* better.

---

## Sign #5: You Feel Hope Again

This one sneaks up on you.

Maybe you laugh more. Maybe you're excited about the weekend. Maybe you smile at someone across the room and your chest doesn't clench, it flutters.

Hope.

It returns quietly. Not in giant declarations of "I'm over it!" but in the soft flickers of interest in life again.

You start to dream again. Plan again. Believe again.

And you don't need a new relationship to feel hopeful.

**Hope is not about finding someone else. It's about finding *yourself*, and realising that life still has beauty, adventure, and love to offer.**

Even better? You're now showing up from *wholeness*, not longing.

And that energy? It's magnetic.

---

## Story: Healing Looked Like This

*Maya* didn't have a dramatic healing moment.

There was no big speech. No epiphany.

Just one evening, six months post-breakup, when she was out for dinner with friends. She caught herself laughing, really laughing, and realised she hadn't thought about her ex all day.

"I used to think about him every five minutes," she said. "And now... it's been hours. I'm just *here*."

That night, she went home, put on a face mask, and danced around her kitchen to Beyoncé.

Not because she was trying to *prove* anything. But because she *felt* it:
 Freedom. Joy. Herself.

That's what healing looks like. Not loud. Not staged. Just *true*.

---

## Healing Is Subtle and Powerful

We tend to think healing will feel big and obvious. But more often, it's quiet.

It's:

- Choosing not to check their profile.

- Saying "no" to things that drain you.

- Saying "yes" to things that light you up.

- Looking back without bitterness, and forward with belief.

These are victories.

Every tiny choice you make to protect your peace, nurture your energy, or invest in your future… that's *healing*.

---

## Confidence Returns Quietly at First

Confidence isn't about strutting through life like you've got it all figured out.

It starts with the inner whisper:

- *I can handle this.*

- *I'm proud of how far I've come.*

- *I trust myself not to settle.*

- *I know who I am now, and that's enough.*

You don't have to scream your healing to prove It.

You just have to *feel it* in your bones.

---

## Your Progress May Not Be Loud, But It's Real

Let this land: **Just because your healing isn't dramatic doesn't mean it isn't profound.**

You are becoming someone more grounded. More discerning. More radiant.
You are shedding what no longer fits.
You are strengthening your emotional muscles.

Your tears counted. Your rest counted. Your quiet moments counted.

And now, your steady, graceful return to joy counts too.

---

## Takeaways to Ground You

Let's reflect on what healing really looks like:

- **Healing is subtle and powerful.** It often arrives in whispers, not declarations.

- **Confidence returns quietly at first.** You begin to feel safe in yourself again.

- **Your progress may not be loud, but it's real.** The quiet wins *matter*.

You're not the same person who started this journey.
You're softer. Stronger. Wiser.
And more *yourself* than ever before.

That's healing. And you're doing it beautifully.

---

## Looking Ahead...

In the next chapter, we'll talk about something tender and often confusing: **When you're ready to date again**. We'll explore how to tell if you're really ready, how to avoid repeating old patterns, and how to date from a place of wholeness, not heartbreak.

You don't have to rush.

But when the time comes… you'll know.

# Chapter 18: When You're Ready to Date Again

There's a moment in every healing journey when a new question starts to surface:

*Am I ready to date again?*

It might come as a whisper at first, when you catch someone's eye in the coffee shop. Or when a friend suggests setting you up. Or when you find yourself re-downloading a dating app "just to browse."

And yet... there's also fear.

- *What if I get hurt again?*

- *What if I mess it up?*

- *What if I attract the same type of person?*

- *What if I'm just lonely?*

These are all fair questions. And asking them doesn't mean you're broken or behind. It means you're *aware*, and that's a very good sign.

**Dating again after heartbreak isn't about finding someone new to fill the void. It's**

**about showing up as a new version of**
*you*.

Let's explore what real readiness looks like, and how to approach dating from *wholeness*, not fear.

---

## How to Know You're Ready

There's no exact timeline for when you'll be ready to date again. Some people need months. Others need a year or more. Some go on a few light dates and realise, *nope, not yet.* All of it is valid.

But here are a few **signs that you may be truly ready**, not just craving distraction or escape:

✅ **You don't feel like you "need" someone to feel complete.**

You're not looking for someone to save you, rescue you, or give you worth. You know you're whole already.

✅ **The thought of dating excites you more than it scares you.**

You might still feel nervous (totally normal), but there's a flicker of curiosity and openness. You're not dragging yourself, *you're drawn forward.*

✓ **You've let go of the old story.**

You're not trying to make your ex jealous, prove your worth, or "win the breakup." You've released the past enough to want something *new*, not a redo.

✓ **You trust yourself to choose differently this time.**

You've done some inner work. You know your patterns. You've learned your lessons. And now, you feel more confident in your boundaries, values, and desires.

If even a few of these resonate… you may be more ready than you think.

---

## Avoiding Rebound Traps

Let's talk about the big, sneaky trap: **the rebound**.

Rebounds aren't *bad*, they're just risky. Because when you date from a place of pain, panic, or pressure, you're more likely to:

- Ignore red flags

- Rush intimacy

- Idealise someone too quickly

- Choose someone who feels familiar, but not necessarily healthy

- Lose yourself in the rush of "being chosen"

And worst of all, a rebound can delay your healing.

Here's the hard truth: *A new relationship won't heal what the last one broke.*

Only *you* can do that. And you already are.

So if you're dating just to numb loneliness, avoid discomfort, or soothe your ego, it's okay to pause.

No judgment. Just honesty.

Give yourself permission to feel lonely *without* rushing into connection.

Because the more comfortable you become with your own company, the more intentional, and powerful, your choices in love become.

---

## Dating From Wholeness, Not Fear

When you're ready to date again, make this your mantra:

**I am choosing love, not chasing it.**

That small shift changes *everything*.

You're no longer dating to prove your worth, you *know* your worth.
 You're not tolerating crumbs, you're waiting for real connection.
 You're not shrinking or pretending, you're showing up *fully yourself*.

That's dating from wholeness.

Here are a few reminders to keep you anchored:

💜 **Date slowly.**

There's no rush. Let things unfold. Slowness reveals truth, fastness often hides it.

💜 **Stay curious, not attached.**

You're gathering information. You're getting to know them, not already imagining wedding hashtags.

💜 **Don't ignore your body.**

If your gut feels tight, your chest feels heavy, or something just feels *off*, listen. Your body always knows.

💜 **Keep your standards, and your softness.**

You don't have to become guarded or cynical. You can be kind and discerning. Open-hearted and self-protective.

You're allowed to want connection. You're also allowed to walk away if it's not aligned.

---

## Story: From Loneliness to Love Again

*Camila* was convinced she'd never want to date again after her breakup. Her trust was shattered. Her heart felt fragile.

But six months into her healing, something shifted. She was dancing in her kitchen one night, cooking for herself, singing along to a playlist she made just for fun, and she realised:

*"I'm not lonely anymore. I'm just… alone. And I'm okay with that."*

A few weeks later, she went on a date, not to fill a void, but because she genuinely wanted to connect. She wasn't attached to the outcome. She wasn't playing games. She showed up as herself.

That date didn't turn into her next big relationship, but it reminded her that her heart was open again. And that she could *trust herself* to choose wisely.

Now, she dates with clarity. With joy. With standards.

Not because she's trying to *get over* anyone. But because she's excited about what's *ahead*.

---

## Love Again, But Don't Rush

There's so much pressure to "move on."
To prove you're okay. To get back out there. To not "waste time."

But you don't owe anyone a timeline.

You don't need to prove you're over it by being in love again.

You can fall back in love with your own life first. Your own body. Your routines. Your rituals. Your peace.

And from that place… love will find you.

It always does.

---

## Choose From Peace, Not Panic

When you date from panic, you'll accept things you know aren't right. You'll chase attention instead of connection. You'll cling to crumbs instead of holding out for what you truly want.

But when you date from *peace*?

You're magnetic.

Because peace says:

- *"I'm not in a hurry."*

- *"I'm happy on my own, and I'm open to more."*

- *"I trust what's meant for me will stay."*

Peace is powerful. It's attractive. And it comes from doing the work you've already done.

You've earned this peace. Now protect it.

---

## You're a New Version of You, And You'll Attract Differently

This is the most beautiful part of post-breakup dating:

**You're not the same person you were before.**

You've grieved. Grown. Let go.

You've built boundaries. Reclaimed joy. Strengthened your intuition.

You've met *yourself* in your darkest hour, and come through with grace.

So when you date again, you'll be dating from that place of growth.

You'll attract differently. You'll respond differently. You'll choose differently.

And the love that aligns with this version of you?

It's going to be so much better than what you lost.

Because it's going to *match* who you are now.

---

## Takeaways to Ground You

Let's reflect on what we've explored:

- **Love again, but don't rush.** There's no timeline, just readiness.

- **Choose from peace, not panic.** Clarity comes from calm, not chaos.

- **You're a new version of you, and you'll attract differently.** Healing reshapes how you show up in love.

You don't have to be fully healed to date again.
But you *do* deserve to date from self-respect, wholeness, and truth.

When the time is right, love will feel different.
Not perfect. Not easy. But *right*.

And you'll know. You'll feel it, not in desperation, but in alignment.

---

## Looking Ahead...

In the next chapter, we'll slow down and reflect on everything this past relationship *taught* you. The good, the hard, the transformative. Because even the most painful endings carry wisdom, and your growth deserves to be seen.

You've made it this far. And what you've learned will shape how you love going forward, in ways that honour both your strength and your softness.

# Chapter 19: Lessons Learned from the Relationship

Every relationship teaches us something.

Even the ones that end in heartbreak.
 Even the ones that weren't "meant to be."
 Even the ones that brought pain, confusion, or loss.

Especially those.

Because growth doesn't just come from getting what we want. It comes from *what we learn when we don't.*

> **This chapter is your moment to gather the gold.**
>
> Not the glittery, romanticised kind. But the *real* gold, found in the reflections, the boundaries learned, the truths uncovered, and the new version of you that emerged.

You don't have to glorify what happened. You don't have to pretend it was all worth it.

But you *can* choose to extract meaning from it.
 You can honour how it shaped you.
 You can turn the pain into power.

And most of all, you can carry forward the wisdom that will serve you in your next chapter.

Let's do this together. Gently. Honestly. Without judgment.

---

## Growth Through Reflection

When we're still reeling from a breakup, reflection can feel too raw.
 But at this stage in your healing journey, something powerful happens: **you gain perspective**.

You start to see the *whole* picture, not just the high highs or the devastating lows.

You start to notice:

- The moments you compromised too much

- The red flags you brushed aside

- The unmet needs you silenced

- The ways you outgrew the relationship long before it ended

- The parts of yourself you're finally reconnecting with

This is not about blaming yourself. It's about reclaiming *clarity*.

Reflection isn't about rewriting history. It's about understanding it.

And from that understanding, you evolve.

> **You become someone who loves more wisely, speaks more honestly, and chooses more intentionally.**

That is growth.

---

## What You Now Know About Love

Let's take a breath and acknowledge what you've come to understand, about love, connection, and emotional safety.

Maybe now you know:

- Love isn't supposed to be confusing.

- If it costs your peace, it's too expensive.

- Real intimacy includes feeling *safe*, not just passionate.

- You deserve someone who shows up *consistently*, not just occasionally.

- Love is a verb, built through action, not just words.

Maybe now you realise that chemistry alone isn't enough. That shared values matter. That you don't have to tolerate neglect or disrespect just to avoid being alone.

These aren't just lessons, they're *truths* born from lived experience. They came at a cost, but now they're yours to keep.

---

## What You Now Know About Boundaries

Most of us don't learn boundaries in theory, we learn them through painful moments where they were missing.

Now you might understand:

- Saying "no" is self-respect, not rejection.

- Overgiving doesn't make someone love you more, it just empties you.

- If someone repeatedly crosses your boundaries, it's not miscommunication, it's a pattern.

- You teach people how to treat you by what you allow and reinforce.

You're not a doormat. You're not "too much."
 You're someone who's learning to protect their energy, their heart, and their standards.

And that's not selfish. It's sacred.

---

## What You Now Know About Yourself

This is the most important part.

What has this breakup, and everything that came before it, taught you about *you*?

Here's what I hope you're beginning to see:

- You are resilient.

- You can survive things you never thought you could.

- You feel deeply, and that's a *strength*.

- You're learning to meet your own needs instead of outsourcing them.

- You are capable of loving again, not just others, but *yourself*.

Maybe you've rediscovered parts of you that got lost in the relationship. Maybe you've uncovered a new voice. A new vision. A deeper connection to your own desires.

Breakups have a way of stripping away what isn't true, so what *is* true can emerge.

And what's emerging now? Is *you*.

---

## A Reflective Exercise: "What This Taught Me"

Take a moment. Breathe.

Write down your answers to these prompts, without editing, judging, or overthinking.

1. One thing I learned about love is...

2. One boundary I now know I need is...

3. One red flag I won't ignore next time is...

4. One quality I truly value in a partner is...

5. One way I've grown through this experience is...

This isn't about getting an "A" in breakup recovery.
It's about being honest with yourself.

And the more honest you are, the more empowered your next chapter will be.

---

## Pain Becomes Power When Reflected On

Pain on its own is just... pain.

But pain that's reflected on? Integrated? Grown through?

That becomes **power**.

Not the aggressive kind. Not the guarded kind.

But quiet, grounded power, the kind that says:

- "I know who I am."

- "I know what I want."

- "I trust myself to walk away from what doesn't align."

- "I don't chase love. I attract it by being fully myself."

That's the power this relationship gave you, not by being perfect, but by being a turning point.

A chapter that shaped you, refined you, and brought you home to yourself.

---

## Every Ending Offers Evolution

Let's say that again:
**Every ending offers evolution.**

You didn't "fail" just because the relationship ended.
You didn't "waste time."
You didn't "lose years."

You gained:

- Clarity

- Strength

- Emotional intelligence

- Boundaries

- Self-awareness

- Resilience

That's not a loss. That's a *becoming*.

The end of the relationship was the beginning of a deeper relationship with *yourself.*

And that's a relationship that will never abandon you.

---

## Your Next Chapter Will Benefit from This One

Everything you've learned, about love, boundaries, self-worth, red flags, green flags, and emotional safety, will guide you going forward.

Your next relationship, if you choose to have one, will be informed by this wisdom.

You'll speak up sooner.
 You'll walk away quicker from what doesn't feel right.
 You'll trust your gut.
 You'll choose from peace, not panic.

And that next chapter? It's already being written. By you.
 Every boundary you set. Every moment of joy you reclaim. Every day you choose healing.

You are not starting over.
You are starting from experience.

And that makes *all* the difference.

---

## Takeaways to Ground You

Let these truths settle in your heart:

- **Every ending offers evolution.** There is always something to learn, carry, and build from.

- **Pain becomes power when reflected on.** You've turned your wounds into wisdom.

- **Your next chapter will benefit from this one.** You are not going backward, you are rising.

You've done the hard work. You've sat with the pain, honoured the loss, and opened yourself to growth.

Now, you walk forward not just healed, but *wiser*, more intentional, and more beautifully *you*.

---

## Looking Ahead...

In our final chapter, we'll come full circle.

You're not just "over it" now. You're *beyond* it.

In Chapter 20, we'll celebrate the freedom, confidence, and joy that comes from doing the deep inner work, and explore how to love yourself as deeply as you once loved them.

Because this journey was never just about getting over someone.

It was always about coming home to *you*.

# Chapter 20: You're Not Just Over It , You're Beyond It

There comes a moment, quiet and powerful, when you realise:

*You're not waiting for the pain to pass anymore.*

You're not counting the days since the breakup.
 You're not holding your breath around memories.
 You're not navigating life with an open wound.

You've made it to the other side.

Not just *over it*.

**Beyond it.**

And that difference matters.

Because "over it" means the crying stopped. The thoughts faded. The pain lessened.

But *beyond it*?
 That means **you've grown through it**. You've expanded. You've integrated the lessons. You've become someone stronger, clearer, and more rooted in self-love than ever before.

> **You're not carrying your heartbreak anymore, you're carrying your healing.**

Let's take this final chapter to honour just how far you've come.

---

## Full-Circle Healing

Think back to Chapter 1.

Remember how you felt?
The shock. The emotional chaos. The desperate questions. The ache in your chest that felt unbearable.

Now breathe into who you are *right now*.

You've faced that darkness. Sat with it. Listened to it. And gently, day by day, you've turned it into light.

Full-circle healing doesn't mean you never think about them again.
It means when you *do*, it doesn't undo you.
It means you remember without crumbling.
It means you see the past *clearly*, but you live in the present, fully.

That's what healing beyond the heartbreak looks like.

You're not stuck in what was.

You're *free* in what is.

---

## Living with Confidence, Hope, and Joy

Here's what your life may look like now, not perfect, but real, rich, and whole:

- You wake up without dread.

- You make decisions that honour your peace.

- You laugh more easily. Smile more genuinely.

- You say "no" without guilt and "yes" without fear.

- You believe in your ability to love, and be loved, again.

You're not trying to *get back* to who you were before the breakup.

You're becoming someone *even better*, because you now know:

- What your boundaries are.

- What your needs are.

- What you will no longer accept.

- And what it truly means to choose *yourself*.

You're living from a deeper well of confidence.
 You're guided by hope that's earned, not naïve.
 And joy? It's no longer something you wait for, *it's something you create*.

That is beyond healing.

That is *thriving*.

---

## Loving Yourself as Deeply as You Once Loved Them

Let's talk about self-love, the kind that lasts longer than any relationship.

You may have once poured your heart into someone who couldn't hold it.

Now? You're learning to hold it yourself.

Every time you speak kindly to yourself…
 Every time you rest without guilt…
 Every time you honour your truth instead of people-pleasing…

You're loving yourself the way you once loved them.

And it's the greatest love story of all.

Because here's what self-love *actually* looks like:

- Setting boundaries, even when it's hard

- Choosing peace over performance

- Believing your needs are valid

- Forgiving yourself, over and over again

- Showing up for your life like you're *worth it* (because you are)

You no longer abandon yourself to be chosen.

You choose *you*, again and again.

And that makes you magnetic, radiant, and unshakably grounded.

---

## Story: From Breakup to Becoming

Let me tell you about *Jordan*.

When their partner left, they were devastated. They felt like their identity had been ripped away. For months, they questioned everything.

But instead of chasing closure or rushing to replace the relationship, Jordan did something different.

They turned inward.

They started journaling. Went to therapy. Took solo trips. Learned to sit with silence. Rebuilt friendships. Said no to things that drained them.

One morning, nearly a year later, they looked in the mirror and whispered:

*"I don't miss them anymore. I miss who I was before I lost myself… and now, I'm back. But better."*

Jordan didn't just get over their ex.

They found *themselves* again.

That's what being beyond it looks like.

---

## You Are Free

Let this truth land:
**You are no longer tethered to the past.**

You've released the fantasy.
You've processed the grief.
You've rewritten the story with honesty.

You're not holding on to what could've been.
You're not stuck in what should've been.

You are here, alive, open-hearted, and ready for what *will be.*

There is no more going back.

Only forward.

---

## You Are Wiser, Stronger, and More Grounded

Through this journey, you've gained:

- Emotional clarity

- Inner strength

- Self-awareness

- Boundaries rooted in self-respect

- A deeper connection to your own voice

You are not who you were when the relationship ended.

You've earned your wisdom. You've softened in the right places and strengthened in the others. You've grown roots, not walls.

You now walk through the world not with fear, but with discernment.
 Not with desperation, but with trust.
 Not with shame, but with self-worth.

You are anchored in *you*.

And that is unshakable.

---

## You Are Ready for What's Next

Whatever comes next, another love, a solo chapter, an unexpected adventure, you're ready.

Because you've done the work. You've faced the hard stuff. You've stayed present when it hurt most.

Now?

You're open.

To new experiences.
 To healthier relationships.
 To deeper self-connection.
 To the kind of love that doesn't confuse you, drain you, or dim you, but *amplifies* you.

You're not just starting over.

You're starting stronger.

## Final Takeaways

Let's close this chapter, and this book, with a few final truths to carry with you:

- **You are free.** The past no longer defines you.

- **You are wiser, stronger, and more grounded.** Your healing is real and earned.

- **You are ready for what's next.** The future is not scary, it's open. And it's yours.

This isn't the end of your story.

It's a *new beginning*, written from truth, strength, and self-love.

## A Note from Me to You 💜

If no one's told you today:
I'm proud of you.

For doing the hard work.
For facing the feelings.
For not giving up on yourself.

You've shown so much courage, and compassion.
And you deserve a love that reflects the work you've done.

But even more than that, you deserve a life that feels like *yours*.

And that life? It starts now.

Here's to love, especially the kind you give yourself.
Here's to healing.
Here's to you.

With warmth and belief in your journey,
**Sophie**

# Conclusion: This Is Your New Beginning

Breakups can feel like endings.
 Sharp, final, life-altering endings.

And in many ways, they are.

They mark the end of routines, dreams, habits, shared futures.
 They unravel the version of life you thought you were building.
 They force you to let go, of someone else, yes, but also of the *story* you were holding onto.

But as you've seen throughout this book… endings are never the full story.

They are also *invitations*.

To come home to yourself.
 To break patterns.
 To rediscover your voice, your worth, your joy.
 To rewrite your relationship with love, from the inside out.

> **This journey wasn't just about getting over them. It was about becoming more fully you.**

You've cried, grieved, questioned, remembered, released, and rebuilt.

You've honoured your pain without letting it define you.

You've replaced shame with clarity.
 Loneliness with strength.
 Regret with wisdom.
 Hope with grounded self-trust.

And now, here you are.

Still standing.
 Still soft.
 Still open.

And that, my friend, is something to celebrate.

---

## You're Not Broken. You're Becoming.

If you take only one thing from this book, let it be this:

**You were never broken. You were breaking open.**

Open to truth.
 Open to healing.
 Open to the next version of your life.

Your heartbreak cracked something, but not your worth.

It cracked the illusion that you had to earn love.
It cracked the patterns that no longer served you.
It cracked open space for a deeper, truer, more empowered version of you to emerge.

And now, you get to live as *her*, or *him*, or *them*, freely, fully, and unapologetically.

---

## Your Heart Will Love Again, But Differently

Yes, you will love again.
But not like before.

You will love with eyes wide open.
With a stronger voice.
With healthier boundaries.
With joy that isn't dependent on someone else's presence.

You'll recognise red flags sooner.
You'll speak your needs more clearly.
You'll choose not from fear, but from peace.

And when love returns, and it will, you won't lose yourself in it.

Because now, you know: *you are already whole.*

---

## This Isn't the End. It's the Rise.

If you're feeling nervous about what's next, let me remind you:

You've already done the hardest part.

You've felt the ache and didn't numb it.
You've sat in the silence and found your strength.
You've faced the questions and found your truth.

From here, things don't necessarily get easier, but they *do* get clearer.

You will wake up lighter.
You will laugh louder.
You will make bolder choices.
You will feel more *you* than ever before.

This isn't just moving on.

**This is rising up.**

---

## Final Words (From My Heart to Yours)

Thank you for walking this journey with me.

I hope these words have been a soft place to land on the hard days.
I hope this book reminded you that heartbreak is not the

opposite of love, it's the consequence of having *loved bravely.*

And I hope you never forget:

- You are worthy of love that feels safe and true.

- You are strong enough to heal anything that tried to break you.

- You are not behind. You are becoming.

- And the best love story you'll ever live… begins with you.

Here's to fresh chapters, new beginnings, and the deep, undeniable beauty of starting over.

You've got this.
 You always have.

With all my heart,
**Sophie Hartman** 💘

## You Made It to the End, Thank You!

If this book spoke to your heart or helped you take even one small step forward, would you mind leaving a **quick review on Amazon**?

Your feedback not only supports my work but also helps others who might be looking for the same guidance you once searched for.

**Your story could inspire someone else's healing.**

# THE EMOTIONALLY INTELLIGENT RELATIONSHIPS SERIES

**Sophie Hartman** is an internationally recognised relationship coach, bestselling author, and emotional wellness expert whose mission is to help people create healthier, more connected, and deeply fulfilling relationships.

Website: **edenrootpress.com**
Instagram: **edenroot.press**

**How to Attract the Right Partner and Find Lasting Love**

**How to Communicate Effectively in Any Relationship**

**How to Make Friends as an Adult**

# THE EMOTIONALLY INTELLIGENT RELATIONSHIPS SERIES

7 Steps to Set Healthy Boundaries

How to Deal with Toxic People

How to Get Over a Breakup and Move On

7 Steps to Reignite the Spark in Your Relationship

How to Build Trust in a Relationship

7 Steps to Resolve Conflicts Without Fighting

# THE EMOTIONALLY INTELLIGENT RELATIONSHIPS SERIES

How to Overcome Shyness in Social Situations

10 Secrets to a Happy and Lasting Relationship

How to Be a Better Listener

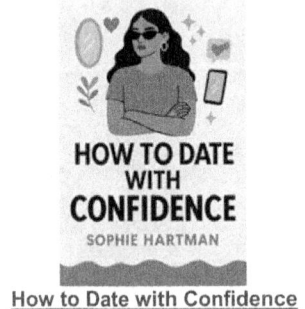

How to Date with Confidence

How to Forgive and Move Forward in Relationships

Printed in Dunstable, United Kingdom

72593281R00121